THE SANTA MONICA MOUNTAINS
RANGE ON THE EDGE

THE SANTA MONICA MOUNTAINS

ANGEL CITY PRESS

RANGE ON THE EDGE

MATTHEW JAFFE

PHOTOGRAPHY BY TOM GAMACHE

For Becky, Nanci and our families, near and far.

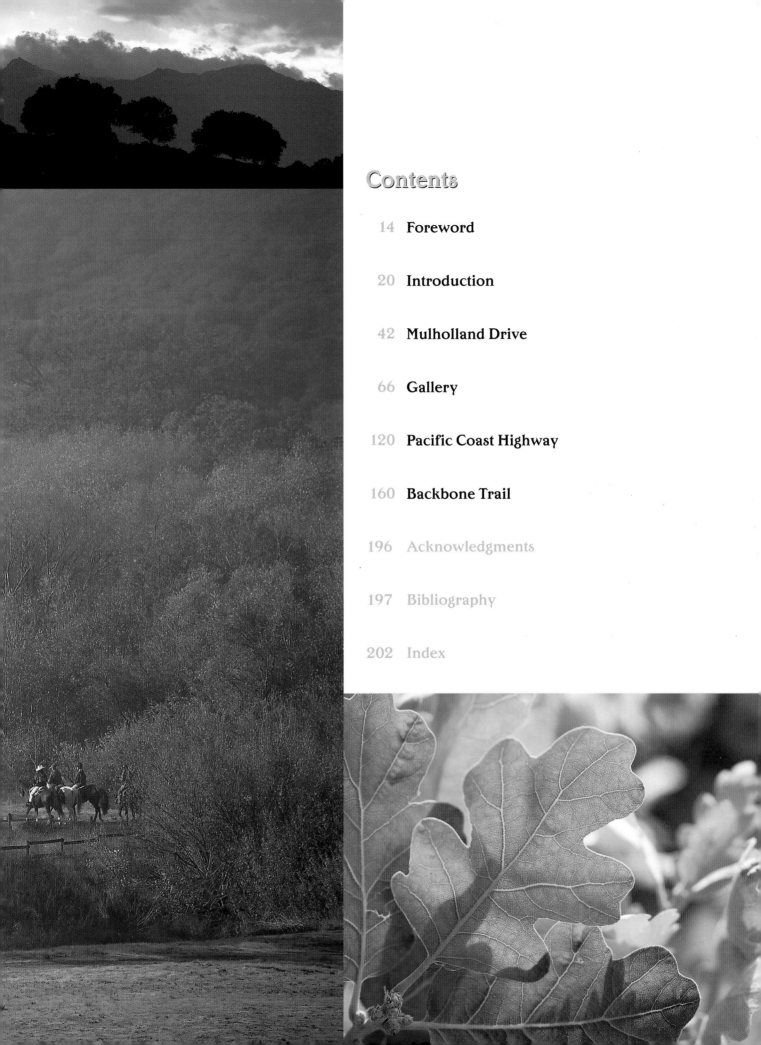

Contents

Foreword

ike so many things in the Santa Monica Mountains, this book began with a fire.

Late morning on November 2, 1993, I was on the phone with photographer Tom Gamache. We hadn't known each other long, but even then our conversations had taken on a familiar free-form structure filled with meandering digressions and non-sequiturs before a return to whatever the subject we were ostensibly discussing. Not surprisingly, I don't remember the conversation's specifics. But I do vividly recall when Tom suddenly declared, "Hey, I'm going. We've got smoke out here." And he was gone.

Tom lived in Calabasas and I was working in an office building off the 405 freeway. I looked out beyond the Sepulveda Pass and across the peaks and ridgelines of Topanga State Park and could see smoke rising into a sky scrubbed blue by Santa Ana winds. This was the start of the Old Topanga Fire.

I didn't get any work done that day. Instead I spent the afternoon at my window watching the smoke grow into a monstrous, dirty cloud fueled by tons of oil-laden chaparral and coastal sage scrub that hadn't burned for decades. For hours the fire surged southward like a wave toward the ocean, propelled by Santa Ana winds.

Tom had arrived in the Santa Monicas in the early 1970s and had photographed many fires. I had covered a few brush fires on the Central Coast but had only been in Southern California for a few years. So the 1993 blaze was my first big Santa Monica Mountains wildfire. Through Joan Didion and Nathanael West, I was well-schooled in the region's literature of disaster and fire's mythic role in Southern California. The Santa Monicas, however, hadn't much figured in my imagination. I can remember marveling at driving from the Fairfax District through Laurel Canyon and miraculously emerging in the parallel universe of Studio City, but I had little sense of the Santa Monicas' geography. And because I was most familiar with the Hollywood Hills, I had no real appreciation for the mountains as a natural place and the miles of wildlands farther west in the range.

Young Sycamore: Dwarfed by its elders, a spindly juvenile grows among the stately, mottled trunks of a sycamore grove at Tapia Park in Malibu Canyon.

The Old Topanga Fire and the following spring when the mountains came back to life with new green growth and fields of rare wildflowers forever changed my sense of the Santa Monicas. Over the years, Tom also changed my perspective on the Santa Monicas by introducing me to the hidden places and lore of a range that in my mind grew from low and anonymous coastal mountains into one of the most intriguing places I had ever known. And ultimately called home.

"A Range on the Edge" has multiple meanings. Geographically the Santa Monicas run along the Pacific and border highly urbanized areas, both in the Los Angeles Basin and along the San Fernando Valley. The complex assemblage of plant communities creates numerous edges within the mountains too, areas of increased biodiversity where unique habitats known as ecotones are formed. On a broader scale, there's a blending of desert and marine influences. On a smaller scale, soil types, topography and microclimates all help to create the range's intricate habitat patterns. Oak forests meet grasslands and chaparral meets coastal sage scrub, allowing animals to take advantage of more than one environment.

There's also a parallel on a cultural level. The interface of the urban and the wild has produced enclaves that neither belong entirely to the city nor to the mountains. These areas have proven to be incubators for creativity, allowing artists to experience both the stimulus of the city and the inspiration of nature, sometimes together and sometimes apart. What has emerged in the Santa Monicas is a kind of cultural ecology, where human activities have influenced the nature of the mountains, and the mountains exert their own influence on the lives of those who live and work in its canyons and along its slopes.

The very beauty of the mountains and their proximity to the city have long made the Santa Monicas one of Southern California's most appealing areas to live in. But development has threatened to compromise the Santa Monicas' continued existence as a viable habitat by burdening the mountains with urbanization. In some places that has destroyed the fragile balance and rhythms that evolved in the range over thousands and thousands of years—an evolution that has made this modest range like nowhere else in the world.

The Grotto: Water trickles down a craggy boulder and into a pool at this secluded spot along the West Fork of Arroyo Sequit below Boney Ridge.

Even as environmental battles over such issues as rainforest protection and global warming continue, a similar struggle has also played out in places closer to where we all live. The landmark efforts that defined earlier generations of environmental activism—Hetch Hetchy, Glen Canyon and Redwood National Park—in our own lifetimes are being waged in less celebrated places with their own environmental significance. And because of their proximity to urban areas, there's a greater immediacy to more people. The battle to save the Santa Monicas and create Santa Monica Mountains National Recreation Area never captured the national or international attention of these other environmental efforts. But consider the growth pressures and sprawl that have overwhelmed much of the natural world in Southern California. The fact that so much of the Santa Monicas has been preserved as open space and wilderness surely must rank as one of the great environmental achievements of our time. Not that there still isn't considerable work ahead.

The establishment of Topanga, Point Mugu and Malibu Creek state parks, as well as the defeat of countless freeway proposals and a planned nuclear power plant in Malibu's Corral Canyon, helped bring the mountains into the public consciousness and ultimately made the creation of Santa Monica Mountains National Recreation Area a reality in 1978. But even then the mountains faced ongoing challenges as the Reagan administration starved it of funds for critical land acquisitions and basic park operations. An effort was even made to de-authorize the park.

It would have been impossible to celebrate the singularity of the Santa Monicas without the work of individuals, organizations and agencies that have spent decades committed to preserving the mountains against what must have often seemed like daunting odds. There was the rise of homeowner and neighborhood associations in the 1950s, the advocacy of Friends of the Santa Monica Mountains in the 1960s and the Sierra Club's March on Mulholland in the 1970s. The local political leadership of Los Angeles City Councilman Marvin Braude and the legislative leadership of Rep. Philip Burton and Rep. Anthony C. Beilenson were critical to the creation of Santa Monica Mountains National Recreation Area. Most recently, the efforts of a diverse coalition led to the defeat of the Ahmanson Ranch development and establishment of the 2,983-acre Upper Las Virgenes Canyon Open Space Preserve in 2003, and in 2005 to the long-held dream of acquiring the King Gillette Ranch in the heart of Malibu Canyon. The battle to save the Santa Monica Mountains has demanded a tireless vigilance.

The park now encompasses seventy thousand protected acres including federal holdings, state parks, properties acquired by the Santa Monica Mountains Conservancy, and lands owned and managed by the Mountains Restoration Trust. Led since 1980 by Joseph T. Edmiston, the Conservancy is a state agency that has helped protect eighty thousand acres both in the Santa Monicas and surrounding ranges to provide public access and preserve the ecological viability of Southern California's surviving wild lands. These acquisitions were made even as the Southern California real estate market made the Santa Monicas some of the most valuable acreage in the country and as local governments gave a green light to development projects on prime acreage,

Eroded Sandstone: Outcroppings along Backbone Trail show horizontal banding, a reminder that this rock began as layers of loose submerged sediment before compressing into stone.

often at densities greater than approved planning standards allow. Especially as it has reached beyond the Santa Monicas, the Conservancy has often generated controversy, not only within the development community but among environmentalists too. That said, seven hundred fifty million dollars has been spent on acquisitions in the mountains, a remarkable reflection of the political and public will that has been brought to bear on the Santa Monicas.

I recently came upon a passage written when Tom and I began to contemplate a Santa Monica Mountains book. Inspired by the classic Sierra Club publications of the 1960s, it read, "We see this book as a manifesto for the Santa Monica Mountains, a document both to enshrine this range as one of the world's unique places and to inspire people to protect it." Pretty lofty stuff, especially for a couple of guys like us.

As the book grew from a fairly straightforward photographic publication into a work with extended text, we also had ambitions both to celebrate the Santa Monicas and to tell the range's complex administrative

and political history. We found, however, that not only does every park and every agency have its story but so does virtually every individual parcel that was eventually brought into the public domain. We opted to take a more impressionistic approach that puts the Santa Monicas' natural history into a broader ecological context and gives the range its due as a center for culture within Southern California.

We hope that this book leads to a deeper appreciation of the Santa Monicas and encourages people to look more closely at these unique mountains. We're convinced that a better understanding of the Santa Monicas can only lead to a commitment to protect the range.

In the end, this book is more personal than political, two visions of the range, one visual and one prose. Just as Tom's photographs capture the areas of greatest beauty and meaning for him rather than serve as a comprehensive survey, I have chosen stories, moments and places that are of the greatest meaning to me. This book is what we know and what we love about the Santa Monica Mountains.

n the upper reaches of a canyon just below Mulholland Drive, a small plaque marks the geographical center of the city of Los Angeles.

Located on the edge of a woodland where native coast live oak trees mingle with eucalyptus from Australia, it's a green and beautiful place, with mockingbirds and mourning doves calling from the trees. In spring the grasses grow tall and the air is cool, fragranced by sage growing on nearby slopes. Vividly orange California poppies and the tiny blossoms of blue-eyed grass with their golden centers sprinkle color into the meadow.

You could walk past this marker countless times and never even notice it. Placed at the base of an oak along the fringes of a spring, it's a small stainless steel plate, more improvised than official. There's none of the grandeur of the brass historical and geographical markers found at other California locations. Instead, the print is off-center and the typeface is informal, the wording no-nonsense and gravely precise.

Point on Balance
of the Plane
of the City of
Los Angeles
34 07 31 N
118 23 56 W
Alt. 920 feet
Allan E. Edwards
12-30-90

Even for those who normally reject the hoariest of Los Angeles clichés, it's difficult to fathom that the center of the country's second largest city would lie here and not at the vortex of a freeway interchange, in a mini-mall parking lot or on a movie studio backlot built to mimic New York. Take your pick of ironies: this is a city where stereotypes die hard.

The marker is at once a curiosity, a bearer of geographic trivia, yet something more. At its core, L.A. is quiet and natural, its biology altered certainly, but

Coyote Silhouette: Even in more developed sections of the Santa Monicas, the yipping and baying of coyotes as darkness approaches is an almost nightly serenade.

nevertheless undeveloped and comparatively unspoiled. It sits on a slope less than a mile from some of the world's most coveted real estate on a protected parcel of land owned by the National Park Service. The city's heart is in the Santa Monica Mountains.

Upon first glance, the Santa Monica Mountains are unremarkable: a whale-shaped forty-six-mile-long range, averaging seven-and-a-half miles across, whose highest point is just over three thousand feet. A range where development has overwhelmed canyons and eaten away at hilltops and ridgelines. A coastal range where the highest peaks may get significant snow only every few decades and with slopes covered by a dense tangle of shrubs, not majestic stands of trees.

While decidedly modest by the standards of the world's great ranges, within Southern California, the Santa Monicas form a distinct sub-region. If, as Carey McWilliams famously described it, Southern California is an island on the land, then the Santa Monicas are an island on the island, distinct in character from the flatlands that surround it.

At the very center of the city, there is still wildness, if not pure wilderness, where native habitat survives to support abundant animal populations. While justly cited as a cautionary tale of overdevelopment, thanks to the Santa Monicas, Los Angeles has perhaps the most untamed acreage of any major world city. In the hills above Hollywood, Griffith Park is the largest municipal park in the United States. Edged by freeways on the city's west side, the so-called Big Wild comprises more than twenty-one thousand acres of unspoiled habitat—the country's largest urban wilderness.

The mountains are home to fires and mudslides, coyotes and rattlesnakes, adding the hint of danger and menace and dark possibility that has long counterbalanced the sunny lightness in the Southern California imagination. The Santa Monicas are a shelter for the otherness that hangs over the city, the sense that there's something out there that we may not have under control.

Where the watered and manicured landscapes of mid-century suburban homes and lavish, late-century faux-Tuscan villas meet tangles of brush on too-steep-to-build slopes, a unique urban-natural interface is formed along a nearly hundred-mile-long front. Much of what people consider iconic Southern California—

Hollywood, Beverly Hills—is actually part of the Santa Monicas. The mountains may invariably be overshadowed by the coast, spiritual home of the endless summer and the California Dream, but the beach too is part of the Santa Monicas, and quite literally so. Its sands are made up of grains worn down from the mountains and carried by creeks and streams to the sea only to be pushed back on land by nearshore currents.

Moonlight and Poppies: Closed for the night, California poppies in Upper Las Virgenes Valley retain their brilliant orange in the fading light.

The range helps define both the geography and history of the city of Los Angeles. The Santa Monicas give L.A. the distinction of being the only major North American city bisected by a mountain range. South of the eastern section of the mountains, the fan-shaped Los Angeles Basin spreads toward the ocean. On the north the mountains hem in the San Fernando Valley, closing it off from the coast. The Los Angeles River begins as seasonal creeks trickle down chaparral-cloaked mountain slopes above the West Valley. From the headwaters, the creeks only briefly flow freely from the mountains before they are confined to concrete flood control channels. Arroyo Calabasas and Bell Creek meet just beyond the grandstands of the football stadium at Canoga Park High School to form the Los Angeles River itself. Once a willow- and sycamore-lined stream that provided water for the original pueblo of Los Angeles, the river, too, is concrete-lined except for a few short stretches where the high water table made such entombment impossible. The river runs east through the San Fernando Valley paralleling the mountains before turning south along the range's eastern edge at Griffith Park. Near downtown the river then enters the Los Angeles Basin, and the site of the original pueblo.

This divide between the valley and the basin— at once geological, climatological and ultimately social— created the fundamental political schism that could have resulted in the breakup of Los Angeles in November 2002. Voters went to the polls to decide whether the Valley would become an independent city. The referendum went down in defeat, as did its possible names: from the Southern California gated-community generic ("Rancho San Fernando"), to the overly literal ("Valley City"), to the wishful and cinematically inspired ("Camelot").

The fact that any of these monikers would even be considered as the name for what would have been the nation's sixth largest city (alas "Valley of the Stars" didn't make it to the ballot) lends a bit of credence to the slam that Southern California is the cultural lightweight champion of the world. The Santa Monicas, however, refute that stereotype. In addition to its regional role, the range has an outsized if largely uncelebrated global significance, both culturally and biologically.

With their balcony-like perspective on the city and ocean and a setting that recalls the Mediterranean, the Santa Monicas have long been the destination of choice for the region's artists and intellectuals. The challenging setting inspired some of the country's most impressive modern architecture, drawing masters including Richard Neutra, Frank Lloyd Wright and Richard Meier. During what writer Cornelius Schnauber called "the greatest cultural diaspora in world history," the mountains became a refuge to a roster of European artists fleeing World War II that included novelist Thomas Mann, playwright Bertolt Brecht and novelist Franz Werfel. And during the 1930s and 1940s the Hollywood Bowl emerged as one of the world's most celebrated concert venues, with many landmark performances, including Sergei Rachmaninoff in one of his final appearances.

Others came to the Santa Monicas during less trying times, drawn to the mountains for their beauty and the natural retreat they offered so close to the city. One

of David Hockney's most famous paintings is his neo-cubist *Mulholland Drive: The Road to the Studio*, showing the road as a rolling ribbon through the hills. And during the 1960s, mountain enclaves such as Laurel Canyon and Topanga Canyon became leading counter-culture communities, bucolic spots that helped inspire the California sound of the Byrds and Joni Mitchell. Neil Young went so far as to declare that his classic *After the Gold Rush* represented "the spirit of Topanga Canyon."

Laurel Canyon may have been the most enduring symbol in the Hollywood Hills during the 1960s but it hardly captured the full and sometimes surreal range of what took place here. Consider just a few snapshots: Richard Nixon while working on his comeback tome *Six Crises* having to hose down the roof of his rented house during one the most devastating fires in Southern California history, the 1961 Bel-Air fire that destroyed

City on the Edge: Buildings trace Wilshire Boulevard as it stretches toward the towers of downtown, while the wild Santa Monicas bump up against ridgeline homes above Brentwood.

four hundred thirty-seven homes. The only meeting between Elvis Presley and the Beatles at The King's Bel-Air mansion following the group's famous performance at the Hollywood Bowl in 1965. Then, four years later, the Charles Manson murders at director Roman Polanski's Benedict Canyon home.

Half a century before the rise of the counter-culture, the mountains also played an early and significant role in the development of Southern California as the capital of the entertainment industry. Offering a nearby and varied terrain, including grasslands, streamside forests and exposed rocky outcroppings, the mountains helped draw early filmmakers to Southern California and turned the small farming community of Hollywood into the hub of one of the world's most visible industries. In the process, the Santa Monicas have been seen by more people around the world than any other mountain range.

Even so, the Santa Monicas remain largely unknown: a non-identified place. Indeed, the Hollywood Sign on Mount Lee may be both the city's and the Santa Monicas' most famous icon, yet it is always described as being in the Hollywood Hills, actually a sub-section of the Santa Monicas. Search the Internet for "Hollywood Hills and Hollywood Sign" and nearly three thousand pages come up; combine the sign with the Santa Monica Mountains and the number is cut to fewer than seven hundred.

While comparisons to the Mediterranean are natural, the Santa Monicas have also evoked allusions to less-expected locations. On his two-thousand-mile horseback ride up the Pacific Coast in 1911, J. Smeaton Chase explored the hills above Little Sycamore Canyon in the western range, and wrote,

Goat Buttes: Morning radiation fog clings to hill contours beneath Malibu Creek State Park's landmark volcanic formations.

The country was strange and un-Californian. In all my wanderings in this varied State I had seen no other region of this kind. It reminded me constantly of the downs of southern England, only that the hills were higher and steeper . . . Now and then a distant glimpse of ocean far below confirmed the resemblance, or some deeply cut cañon carried the mind a little farther afield to the combes of Dorset or Devon.

Specific as Chase's comparison is, there's also a universality to the landscape that allows people to accept the Santa Monicas as just about anywhere a filmmaker says it is. Having doubled for wartime Korea, Imperial Siam and the Old West, to name a few roles, the

Santa Monicas are a character actor of a landscape—even a faceless extra—rather than the star that John Ford made of Utah's Monument Valley in his classic westerns. During the 1960s, that versatility was evidenced in Franklin Canyon. Located a short distance from the geographic marker, Franklin Canyon Lake was seen by millions weekly as that most American of places, the fishing hole, in the opening of *The Andy Griffith Show*. The canyon also managed to double for High Sierra forests in TV's *Bonanza* and as post-D-Day France in the World War II series *Combat*. In these same years, it gained a permanent place in pop iconography as the shooting location for the cover of the 1966 Rolling Stones album *Big Hits (High Tide and Green Grass)*, a shot where the dour light, treeless rock-strewn banks and grim stares appear more Stepney than Studio City. Also that year, Simon and Garfunkel were portrayed feeling groovy and

the striking features of the lake is the lush forest of deodar cedars and coast redwoods along its shores. None of these trees, however, is native to the Santa Monicas; the trees were instead planted in 1940 when the Works Project Administration made improvements here.

The artifice of Franklin Canyon hardly seems to bother its park-starved visitors; Los Angeles has 4.2 acres of city parkland per thousand residents while most American cities range from 6.25 to 10.5 acres per thousand residents. Families of Orthodox Russian Jews from West Hollywood come to picnic in the shade of the forest. Hardcore, heartrate-monitored trail runners from Beverly Hills challenge themselves on the narrow, steep trails that climb from the canyon bottom and onto the chaparral-covered slopes. Hikers move at a more sedate pace and bird-watchers may barely move at all as they scan the scrub for such distinctive birds as the western tanagers.

To discuss the Santa Monicas' role as a haven for culture and recreation reflects both the range's appeal as a place to live and the degree to which large portions of the mountains have been settled and urbanized. It is not, however, to suggest that the very nature of the mountains has been sublimated to its cultural role. While human beings have reshaped and reinterpreted the mountains, the mountains are also able to unleash an astounding capacity for destruction, thus reasserting the natural order. Development can destroy the mountains but the mountains can come back to destroy development. The often tense interplay of the urban and natural in the Santa Monicas gives these mountains their distinct character, and it gives this book a degree of urgency as well.

With seventy thousand protected acres sprawling over one hundred fifty-four thousand acres in the mountains, Santa Monica Mountains National Recreation Area is the largest urban national park in the world. It's a ragged, quilt-like assemblage of federal and county lands and state parks created in the 1960s that offered the range its first significant protections, as well as parcels owned by the state's land acquisition agency for the range, the Santa Monica Mountains Conservancy. The park faces a unique set of challenges as it balances the leisure needs of millions of people (including beach areas, there were thirty-three million visitors in 2004)

rushing excitedly down a rainy country road through a green forest on the cover of *Sounds of Silence*. With their New York roots, you would have to assume the forest is somewhere on the East Coast, but it too was shot in Franklin Canyon.

Like many sections of the range, Franklin Canyon is a hybrid of natural and created environments. Its beauty and very existence as a quasi-wild place is the paradoxical result of its role serving the development that surrounds it.

For one thing, the lake itself is not natural. As part of the vast project that carried water nearly three hundred miles from the Owens Valley to Los Angeles, in 1916 William Mulholland (for whom Mulholland Drive, the winding road that crosses the range, is named) completed the canyon's two reservoirs, which became the first in the city to store water from the project. One of

Cheeseboro Spring: Non-native mustard blankets the rolling hills of Cheeseboro Canyon while the green of coast live oaks traces the course of the creek.

with the protection of habitat and Native American sites that date back ten thousand years—all while often-insensitive development continues to push into the range. This is not a classic national park in the sense of Yosemite or the Grand Canyon.

The beauty of the Santa Monicas is ultimately more subtle and so, too, is its significance. These mountains are considered the finest surviving example of Mediterranean habitat in North America. Of the world's eight major biological communities, which include deserts and rainforest, the Mediterranean bióme (also known as broad-leafed evergreen forest) is actually the smallest and most endangered. Scattered around the world on five continents, the biome only covers two percent of the Earth's land area and exists in narrow coastal bands along the Mediterranean itself, Chile, southwest Australia, South Africa and Southern California. Worldwide, just eighteen percent of the original acreage

survives and the Santa Monicas may be the most endangered of that which remains.

The pressures on this habitat are understandable. With its mild temperatures, wet winters and dry summers, the Mediterranean climate is without a doubt the most benign in the world. Those who move to the Santa Monicas also go there desiring views and proximity to nature. But based on much of the development in the Santa Monicas, few people understand the character, uniqueness and fragility of the range's natural system. For one thing, the inevitability of wildfires is routinely ignored.

In the Santa Monicas, the Mediterranean designation is actually a catchall term for twenty-six unique natural communities that exist in the range. The range has elevations from sea level to over three thousand feet. A complex geology with its numerous folds and canyons and a unique east-west orientation combine with a proximity to the ocean to create survival opportunities for a broad range of plants and animals. Common in the Pacific Northwest, populations of broad-leafed maples grow in isolated stands in cool, well-watered canyons, the descendents of forests that existed here in wetter and chillier times. One of the range's most iconic trees is the valley oak, but the Santa Monicas actually represent the southernmost limits of its range.

The valley oak is not the only species on the edge; twenty endangered or threatened plants and animals live in the Santa Monicas, a range where black bears wandering in from nearby ranges and resident mountain lions occasionally make their way into suburban backyards and onto the evening news. An estimated four hundred fifty vertebrate species live here, up to and including increasing numbers of humans. In the Santa Monicas, biodiversity is freeway close.

A Chronological Journey Through the Santa Monicas

For many Southern Californians, the Santa Monica Mountains are not just geographically central to their lives but spiritually, emotionally, politically and intellectually as well. There is a community of people whose lives revolve around the mountains. They follow rainfall totals and wildflower blooms, new construction projects and the latest land acquisition. They swap arcane literary references to the mountains and can look at a ridge and say the exact year it burned, locate in an instant a bend in a road where a car commercial was shot, or identify a peak glimpsed in the background of a movie filmed in the 1930s.

Such devotion usually doesn't manifest itself as epiphany but instead develops and deepens over time. The relative compactness of the Santa Monicas gives a

Sand Verbena: While a related species is commonly seen in Southern California deserts, the Santa Monicas' only sand verbena is found on beaches.

Dodder and Buckwheat: A tangle of dodder entwines buckwheat. Dodder is a parasite species that feeds off the carbohydrates of a variety of mountain plants.

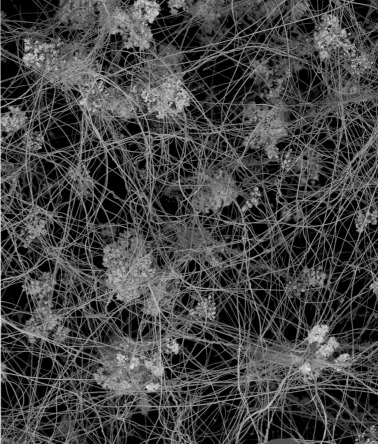

Saddle Peak: Tilted sandstone slabs give 2,805-foot Saddle Peak its distinctive profile and take on a golden glow during late afternoon.

sense that these mountains can be fully known, yet, like any chunk of Earth, the story spans not just geography, but time too. And as essential as it is to provide a snapshot of what the mountains are today, it is hard to understand what they have become without also seeing what they have been along the way.

One of the enduring pop-culture myths of California is that one day a cataclysmic earthquake will cause the state to plunge into the Pacific. The reaction ranges from the tsk-tsking of the morality police that this disaster will have resulted from the godless ways of the populace to the ever-resilient optimism of real estate speculators who look longingly east at all that future coastal property on the Nevada border—as though geology and/or God's wrath will neatly follow state lines.

Thus far, at least in our lifetimes, the Pacific has yet to swallow up Southern California. But that hasn't

always been the case. The Santa Monicas have spent plenty of time underwater and the mountains we see today are the result of these periodic inundations.

It's important to bear in mind that the current continental configuration bears little resemblance to the Earth's geography as the materials that would ultimately comprise the Santa Monicas were being created. The terrestrial world existed as one gigantic landmass known as Pangea up to two hundred million years ago when it divided into two supercontinents, Laurasia and Gondwana. North America, until about sixty-five million years ago, consisted of two islands divided by a body of water known as the Bearpaw Sea.

Considering that the Earth is an estimated 4.5 billion years old, having been uplifted from the sea most recently about three to four million years ago, the Santa Monicas are a young range. Along with the San

Ceanothus Slopes: Fragrant and delicate, the blossoms of ceanothus sprinkle color into the chaparral beneath a sandstone outcrop. Displays typically begin late winter.

Bernardino, San Gabriel and Santa Ynez mountains and the Northern Channel Islands, the Santa Monicas are part of the Transverse Ranges, so named for their atypical east-west orientation; with the exception of Utah's Uinta Mountains, all other major North American mountains trend north-south.

The Santa Monicas sit on the Pacific Plate near the boundary with the North American Plate, the demarcation traced by the San Andreas Fault. The Pacific Plate is gradually moving northward. Los Angeles may not fall into the sea, but it will be San Francisco's neighbor in nine million years.

For more than two hundred million years, the heavier Pacific Plate slid under the North American plate before the plates began sliding past each other, as they do today, with one moving north and the other south. As a result, mountains were from time to time forced up,

folded and faulted. Then between about twenty and five million years ago, lateral movement and pressure along the plates caused the earth's crust to rotate clockwise about one hundred degrees, which accounts for the Transverse Ranges' orientation.

To date the mountains at a few million years old only tells part of the story. Considered the most geologically diverse of the Transverse Ranges, the Santa Monicas are actually comprised of rock ranging from one hundred fifty-four to four million years old. The oldest is known as Santa Monica Slate. It began as subsea mud before pressure hardened this loose sediment into shale. About one hundred million years ago, it turned to slate as intruding molten material, seeping toward the surface from the Earth's mantle, heated it. That material eventually hardened as well, forming the mountains' core. This intrusion, known as a batholith, is

sometimes referred to by the cinematic name Hollywood Granite.

The intruding rock pushed the nascent range up above the water's surface, where it was subjected to erosional forces on land. The land eventually subsided and was again inundated by the sea. The water deposited additional marine sediment that combined with debris from erosion when the land was above the surface. Eventually compressed into rock, these materials formed a rock formation known as the Tuna Canyon Formation, which overlays the older Santa Monica Slate.

Additional uplift and erosion followed by subsidence and deposition cycles produced new rock formations. Evidence of the range's oceanic origins are common in the Topanga Formation. In his classic account, *Up and Down California*, William H. Brewer was struck by the wealth of marine fossils found at high elevations in the range. He visited the Santa Monicas while working on the geological survey of California and wrote of a shell-packed ridge two thousand feet above sea level near Triunfo Ranch in the western range:

> The ridge was strewn with them, as thick as any seabeach I have ever seen and in as good preservation—oyster shells by the cartload, clam shells . . . I cannot describe my feelings as I stood on that ridge, that shore of an ancient ocean. Who shall tell how many centuries, how many decades of centuries, have elapsed since these rocks resounded to the roar of breakers and these animals sported in their foam.

As a result of repeated episodes of uplift and inundation, the mountains consist of many tens of thousands of feet of sedimentary rock. It would be simple to describe the underlying terrain as a layer cake of rock but the picture is more complex. For one thing, not all the material was deposited by the sea. About seventeen million years ago, a huge Hawaiian-type volcano grew from the bottom of the ocean to more than five thousand feet above sea level. This volcano's rock is known as the Conejo Volcanics and is primarily found at the central to western section of the range. Nor do the rock layers sit in neat, horizontal bands. At Calabasas Peak, the twenty-million-year-old sandstone tilts at angles approaching ninety degrees.

This pattern of uplift, erosion, inundation and deposition continues today. The mountains are rising at the rate of about 1.7 inches per year, although seismic events sometimes accelerate the process; the 1994 Northridge Earthquake, for example, elevated nearby mountains in an instant.

The mountains' geology set the stage for a unique biological story to play out, where huge climatic and botanical variations occur over short distances. The Santa Monica's east-west orientation creates extensive areas of north-facing slopes on the range's inland side and south-facing grades on the Pacific side. South-facing slopes receive longer and more direct sunlight than north-facing slopes. However, in the Santa Monicas this simple distinction is complicated because its south-facing slopes benefit from moisture from fog while the north-facing side tends to be hotter. As you drive from the coast to the San Fernando Valley via Topanga Canyon Boulevard, summer temperatures can vary forty degrees in less than ten miles.

Nor are the two faces of the mountains uniform in contour. Because the Santa Monicas are a young range with comparatively low rates of precipitation, they still feature many jagged outcrops that have not yet been sanded down to a more rounded outline. Rugged and steep, the Santa Monicas are incised by forty distinct watersheds, although only the fourteen-mile-long Malibu Creek cuts all the way through the range, creating a gorge nearly two thousand feet deep in sections. It's probably the most dramatic example of the erosional forces at work in the mountains.

The wide variations in soils, topography and climate in the mountains have had a profound impact on its biodiversity. Plant communities from coastal salt marshes to cactus scrub survive in the mountain zone. In shaded moist grottoes, Venus maidenhair ferns can create a lush, almost rainforest-type setting while a hundred yards away the spear-like leaves of the chaparral yucca (also known as Our Lord's Candle) are a reminder of the range's arid character.

The dominant plant community in the Santa Monicas is chaparral, the so-called elfin forest. Chaparral is a third-generation term, according to historian and fire expert Stephen J. Pyne, and was derived

Last Light of Day: The Channel Islands appear squeezed between purple skies and purple ocean as the sun drops beneath winter storm clouds.

originally from the Basque *chabarra*, a reference to a scrub oak in the Pyrenees. The Spanish converted the term to *chaparro*, which they used to describe the brush community that they found in California, where the word evolved to chaparral in English usage.

Scrub oak is actually just one component of chaparral, a collection of plants that thrives on gravelly slopes and in a climate with cool, wet winters and hot, dry summers when no rain may fall at all: the very conditions that define the Mediterranean climate. To cope with these conditions, common chaparral species such as chamise and ceanothus feature small, thick leaves, with a waxy coating to limit evaporation. Their root systems are designed to maximize the moisture that is available, thanks to a deep tap root and roots near the surface that extend out well beyond the plant's canopy.

Another defining trait of the chaparral community is its adaptation to fire. Fire is part of the natural cycle in the mountains and while devastating in the short term, it's also key to the long-term health of the ecosystem. Most chaparral plants are so adapted to fire that within days of burning, they re-sprout directly from an underground root crown, even if the portion of the plant above the surface has been incinerated. Many chaparral plants have seeds that only germinate after exposure to the intense heat of fires. Uncommonly high in oils to help limit loss through evaporation, chaparral plants carry with them the source of their own destruction and rebirth. Introduce fire and those oils burn hot and fast. The fuel load on an acre of mature chaparral is estimated to be equal to fifteen hundred to two thousand gallons of gasoline.

"It burns like a torch of fat," wrote Francis M. Fultz in his 1923 paean to chaparral, *The Elfin Forest*.

Fultz rhapsodized about the wonders of chaparral but had to acknowledge that this brushy and all but impenetrable plant community is an acquired taste.

Everything about it was so new and strange that I almost felt as if I were in another world. Of the brush of which it was composed, there was scarcely a familiar form, and it was all so harsh and unyielding that it aroused a certain feeling of hostility within me.

The Santa Monicas' climate was once considerably warmer and wetter than it is now. The ancestors of the chaparral community, however, were present in the understory of California conifer forests of that time. But when conditions grew drier and fires increased as the Mediterranean climate pattern became established about ten million years ago, they were able to survive and spread while many woodland species could not. Chaparral-type plants then living in Mexico also began to move north and now comprise a major portion of the California floristic province.

Climate is even less fixed than geology and the area has continued to undergo considerable weather variation. The Santa Monicas were never actually covered by Ice Age glaciers but did experience much cooler conditions as recently as twelve thousand years ago. The glaciation had another significant impact on the area: With water locked up in the ice, the ocean level dropped dramatically. The Channel Islands, the western geological extension of the Santa Monicas, were fused into a single landmass and the gap between the islands and mainland was reduced to just a few miles. Sea level was three hundred feet lower even as recently as twenty thousand years ago.

Humans came to California roughly thirteen thousand years ago and their occupation of the Santa Monicas is estimated to have started ten thousand years ago. These earliest residents encountered a wildlife com-

A Wilder Shore: Pacific Coast Highway runs along cuts made into the mountains as they drop to the Pacific at a driftwood-strewn beach near the mouth of Sycamore Canyon.

munity that was in decline. The climate was growing warmer and drier, and larger grazing animals once common in the area, such as mammoths, were gone. Their absence in turn led to the extinction of their predators, primordial carnivores including dire wolves and saber-toothed cats.

Over time, California's Native Americans diversified into a remarkable range of cultures and linguistic groups. As many as eighty languages were spoken in six major groups, with more than one hundred tribes in territories ranging from the desert to the coast. By the time the Spanish arrived in the sixteenth century, California's population was about three hundred thousand, a comparatively high density for North America at the time.

The Santa Monicas eventually became a meeting ground of two major Southern California Indian cultures. The better known, the Chumash, ranged from the Central Coast south to Malibu and its canyons. Based on burial practices and artifacts, the Chumash culture emerged in the range almost from the time people first arrived in the mountains and continued to evolve over the ensuing millennia. The Tongva (or Gabrieleño) ranged in the eastern part of the mountains, into the Los Angeles Basin and out to Catalina and San Clemente islands. While there was considerable cultural overlap, the two came from separate language traditions. The Chumash spoke a Hokan dialect; Hokan is the oldest language group and its speakers extended all the way up the coast and into far Northern California. The Tongva spoke a Takic (or Shoshonean) language similar to those spoken by desert tribes.

There's a tendency to idealize these early California peoples and to present their world as an unchanging, uncomplicated Eden-like paradise. But things were hardly static, especially over such a long period of time. Although the climate was mild and food was comparatively plentiful, these early peoples still had to contend with changing conditions that could result in periodic shortages. Over time new strategies and technologies were developed that changed their relationship to the local environment.

The Tongva and Chumash understood the role of fire in the native ecosystem and used it to burn areas and encourage the production of seed-bearing plants. One of the pivotal changes in their early societies occurred roughly eight thousand years ago, as acorns became a staple of their diet as well as that of other California Indians. Although plentiful, acorns were time-consuming to process and bitter to the taste. The development of the mortar and pestle allowed for more efficient processing of acorns into a flour that could then be leached to remove tannins.

Because acorns could be collected and stored, they brought new stability to food supplies, which meant that people could live less nomadic lives and settle into more permanent communities. With less time spent on the move, societies gradually became more politically and culturally complex and new inventions could be developed. In the case of the Tongva and the Chumash, a monetary system evolved using shell beads. And the *tomol*, a plank boat made of redwood that washed ashore and tar found on beaches, was refined by about 650 A.D. into an impressive craft used to hunt at sea and to trade with villages on the Channel Islands. The tomols' owners and builders formed an elite within Chumash and Tongva society, and reflected the hierarchical structure that emerged over time in these communities.

It's difficult to imagine the reaction on the day in 1542 when a far grander vessel captained by Spanish explorer Juan Rodriguez Cabrillo appeared off the Santa Monica Mountains coast. Cabrillo spent little time along this shore on his way north but left his mark. He made reference to Mugu, a Chumash village along the coast although the word was probably *muwu*, meaning beach. Thus, thanks to such spots as Point Mugu and Mugu Lagoon at the range's western edge, the Santa Monicas apparently have the distinction of bearing "the oldest California name in continuous written use" according to the book *California Place Names: The Origin and Etymology of Current Geographical Names*.

Cabrillo also described a village with large houses along the coast, from where a number of tomols, each carrying as many as twelve or thirteen people, rowed out to meet him. He came ashore at the village and took possession of the land in the name of Spain, dubbing the settlement *Pueblo de las Canoas* (literally Village of the Canoes). While scholars have historically placed this site further up the coast, either near Point Mugu or Ventura, others believe that the village site could have been at Malibu Lagoon at the mouth of

Traces of the Past: Little remains from the Chumash and Tongva cultures that thrived for thousands of years, but these grinding holes are a reminder of their longtime presence.

Tri-peaks Panorama: Beyond the pyramid-like silhouette of Goat Buttes, Mulholland Highway's Seminole Spings Overlook looks east toward the Santa Monicas' fellow Transverse Range, the San Gabriels—the most distant ridge.

Malibu Canyon.

Ronald Rindge, descendent of the onetime owners of the *Rancho Topanga Malibu Sequit,* sought to have the Malibu Lagoon area officially designated as the site of the pueblo. Rindge argues that the pueblo was the first and only site in California where Cabrillo made a documented claim of possession in the name of Spain; therefore this spot on the edge of the Santa Monicas would constitute the formal beginning of the Spanish conquest of California. And even though it would be more than two hundred years until the Spanish returned to these mountains, Cabrillo's arrival marked the beginning of the end for the range as a pure California place and was a harbinger of the demise of its Native Californian cultures.

In response to British adventurism and Russian expansionism down the West Coast driven in part by the pursuit of sea otter pelts, Spain's King Carlos III decided to colonize *Alta California* and establish a mission at Monterey. The expedition left Mexico in January 1769 and that summer a division led by Gaspar de Portolá reached the Santa Monicas. He touched on the far southeastern edge of the range at what is now Elysian Park,

then headed west via an Indian trail that was eventually to become Wilshire Boulevard.

An advance party scouted for a route along the coast but, blocked by the mountains' precipitous drop to the ocean, they returned to the main group. The expedition instead headed north through a canyon that was later to become known as Sepulveda Pass. The party dropped down into the San Fernando Valley, passing the present-day site of the interchange of U.S. Highway 101 and Interstate 405. Like Cabrillo before him, Portolá's foray into the Santa Monicas was brief; the mountains were a barrier to overcome, not a place of promise to explore. Still, Portolá left a lasting imprint. While Padre Juan Crespi, who kept a diary of the trip, referred to the range as *Sierra de la Conversion,* Portolá is credited with naming these mountains in honor of St. Monica, the mother of St. Augustine and the patron saint of alcoholics, abuse victims and wives. The naming of *Sierra de Santa Monica* is believed to have occurred on a second Portolá expedition that left San Diego in April 1770. The explorers followed the same route, which would have put them in the vicinity of the Santa Monicas on May 4, the saint's traditional feast day.

In 1776 when Juan Bautista de Anza made his journey from Tubac, Arizona, to the site of today's San Francisco, his route varied slightly through the Santa Monicas. Instead of the Sepulveda Pass, his party traveled through the current location of Griffith Park and then stayed along the northern flank of the range. The party most likely camped in Malibu Canyon at a spot they dubbed *Agua Escondida*.

De Anza's stay in the Santa Monicas was also brief and it was the establishment of the missions at San Gabriel and San Fernando that marked the start of a permanent Spanish presence in Southern California. Although neither was in the immediate vicinity of the Santa Monicas, the Chumash and Tongva in the mountains tragically came under Spanish domination. Forced labor, religious conversion through physical abuse and the introduction of European diseases into the population destroyed the fabric of native society in the mountains.

While a small number of Chumash continued to live in scattered settlements in the mountains' backcountry, the Spanish began to divide the range into enormous land grants. The first, 6,647 acres, at what is now Griffith Park, was granted to a member of the de Anza party, Jose

Vicente Feliz, in 1796. In 1804, 13,316 acres in Malibu was granted to Jose Bartolome Tapia. This land grant, *Rancho Topanga Malibu Sequit*, remained intact into the twentieth century under the Rindge family.

Spanish rule in California came to an end when Mexico declared independence from Spain in 1821. Under Mexico, the rate of land grant distribution increased but the Santa Monicas were hardly a settled place. Smugglers seeking to avoid Mexican import restrictions docked in remote coves and transported goods through the mountains. Cattle-grazing was the main activity in the Santa Monicas, which greatly accelerated the rate of environmental change. One of ranching's consequences was the accidental introduction of numerous non-native plants, which has resulted in huge impacts that continue to this day. The golden grasses of summer that provide the backdrop for the oak woodlands are almost all of European extraction.

Mexican rule of California was short-lived and the Santa Monicas provided the stage for its demise. The U.S.-Mexican War began in 1846 after the U.S. annexation of Texas the previous year. The California phase of the war concluded after decisive American victories in Southern California and the signing, on January 13, 1847, of a treaty between famed and sometimes notorious American explorer and adventurer John C. Fremont and Mexican General Andres Pico at a site in the Cahuenga Pass, the most prominent gap for travel through the eastern Santa Monicas.

The pact between Fremont and Andres Pico was known as the Treaty of Campo de Cahuenga and ended conflict in California. While the official end of the war came with the signing of the Treaty of Guadalupe Hidalgo in 1848, for all intents and purposes California became a part of the United States on the porch of an adobe in the Santa Monica Mountains.

Through the more than one hundred fifty years that the Santa Monicas have been under American control, the pace of change has accelerated drastically. Whereas an estimated thirteen hundred Chumash and Tongva were living in the Santa Monicas prior to the Spanish *entrada*, there are now hundreds of thousands of people living in the mountains today.

There is much to lament, from the approval of insensitive developments in pristine areas that have occasionally required heroic fire-fighting efforts, to the loss of the once prodigious run of steelhead through Malibu Creek and other Santa Monica Mountains watersheds due to stream degradation. None of these issues can be ignored and certainly there are places in the Santa Monicas where the natural world has been all but overwhelmed.

But as often as one might feel a deep sense of loss and regret when standing along a steep, freeway-wide road climbing from the valley virtually to the high ridgeline to service a gated community of multi-million-dollar homes, there are still places where the mountains feel as fresh as they did to the earliest travelers and settlers.

Serrano Canyon sits on the western end of the range in the Boney Mountain State Wilderness. To the northeast, the jagged volcanic rock of three-thousand-foot-tall Boney Ridge looms more than twenty-five hundred feet above the sloping valley. Hillsides of chaparral surround the valley's grasslands, which in spring come alive in a palette of infinite greens. A riparian corridor of oak, willow and sycamore cuts across the valley. There are no buildings, just the remnants of a ranch less notable for its age than the fact of its demise.

Set down behind a peak that rises to fourteen hundred feet in less than two miles from the ocean, the valley is cut off from the nearby Pacific. The valley is hidden but the ocean still finds it as fog begins to drift through a canyon opening and curls over the high ridge in a slow-motion cascade.

The fog is the only thing that intrudes from beyond the valley. There's no hint of the motorcyclists and commuters racing up and down Pacific Coast Highway. The sensation is the same as that described by author William H. Brewer almost one hundred fifty years earlier when he stopped at a spot nearby in the Santa Monicas: "A feeling of awe came over me. Around me rose rugged mountains; no human being was within miles of me to break the silence."

Earth's Shadow: From an overlook above Point Mugu State Park's Serrano Canyon, the Earth's shadow is visible as a line of blue above the ridgeline.

Mulholland Drive

The Santa Monica Mountains rise abruptly from the gap where the Los Angeles River separates the range from the San Rafael Hills to the east. The Golden State Freeway edges the base of the mountains and old neighborhoods climb up its steep slopes. Here the Santa Monicas nearly reach downtown Los Angeles. Chavez Ravine, a home to Dodger Stadium, is a hollow in the southeast corner of the Santa Monicas, and the Art Deco Figueroa Tunnels on the Pasadena Freeway were cut through a finger of the range in 1931.

From this eastern extreme of the range west to the Sepulveda Pass, the Santa Monicas form a unique, if overdeveloped, urban district, a hybrid of natural and man-made environments. Eighty years of intense development have chased the natural ecosystem to a few large parcels of open space and to numerous fragmented patches of native vegetation too steep for building. The mountains here survive less as a cohesive, natural system than as isolated remnants, such as Runyon Canyon above Hollywood.

The canyon is named for Carman Runyon, a successful Eastern coal magnate who bought the canyon as a hunting-and-riding retreat. It's one of the series of canyons, including Nichols, Laurel, Benedict, Coldwater and Beverly Glen canyons, cut into the southern slopes of the Santa Monicas overlooking the Los Angeles Basin. The hundred-thirty-acre tract begins off Fuller Avenue, where a neighborhood of mostly generic postwar apartment buildings ends just a few blocks north of Hollywood Boulevard. Once known as No Man's Canyon, Runyon is one of the most intensively used areas in the Santa Monicas, more of an everyman's canyon now, drawing from both the densely populated Hollywood flats and the more rarified climes of the hilltop enclaves near its upper reaches.

The lower canyon was once the estate of A&P grocery chain heir George Huntington Hartford. He had purchased the property from the world-renowned Irish tenor John McCormack. Over the years a variety of Hollywood stars lived here: McCormack rented his estate, dubbed San Patrizio, to Charles Boyer and Janet

Hollywood Habitat: Although the most developed section of the Santa Monicas, the Hollywood Hills still have many areas that support native vegetation, such as toyon whose berries ripen in winter.

Gaynor and for a period Errol Flynn crashed in Hartford's pool house. The estate was eventually demolished to make way for development that never came, and all that survives are garden terraces, some foundations and overgrown gardens with impressive Canary Island palms. With its echoes of Old Hollywood, these remains carry the stature of antiquity—at least by a Southern California time scale—and the grounds have the moody, ancient aspect of a Roman villa's ruins.

Steep trails climb from the canyon floor to a narrow ridge that ascends all the way to Mulholland Drive. The elevation affords a clear look at the disconnect between the mountains and the surrounding urban environment. On a spring afternoon, yellow flowers bloom on prickly pear cactus and a tower of creamy blossoms rises from a chaparral yucca. The purple sage is in bloom, suffusing the air with an aromatic blast and a red-tailed hawk rides the thermals above the canyon floor. It's an almost iconic Santa Monica Mountains scene; that is, until sirens along Hollywood Boulevard redirect the gaze to the city that begins its surge from the base of the slopes. Billboards loom over the boulevard and an assortment of Hollywood landmarks are visible: the Capitol Records building, Grauman's Chinese Theater and the Cinerama Dome. As summer approaches, the purple haze of jacaranda traces the course of city streets and to the east, processions of houses line up on ridges as they descend from the mountains toward Hollywood. Runyon Canyon is surrounded.

Urbanized as it is, the eastern end of the range is also home to the two largest parks in Los Angeles. Together, Griffith Park and Elysian Park comprise nearly five thousand acres or almost one-third of the city's total parkland. Portions of both are developed as traditional urban parks, but considering their proximity to the downtown of the country's second-most-populous city and their tenuous ties to the remainder of the Santa Monicas and the nearby San Gabriel Mountains, they remain remarkably wild places. Coyotes thrive, and in 2004 a mountain lion managed to thread its way through a web of channelized waterways, apparently venturing from the San Gabriels to take up residence, at

least for awhile, in Griffith Park. With the park's sizeable herd of mule deer, the lion wouldn't have gone hungry.

Griffith Park embodies the contradictions of both the Santa Monicas and the city of Los Angeles as a whole. Here on the fringes of Hollywood and just a few miles from downtown Los Angeles is a more than five-square-mile area of steep slopes, volcanic outcrops and rugged canyons, as well as such major cultural venues as the Greek Theater, the Museum of the American West and the Griffith Observatory, site of James Dean's knife fight in the 1955 film *Rebel Without A Cause*.

Suburban neighborhoods of classic ranch houses and the estates of the early Hollywood elite edge its boundaries. For residents of such adjacent communities as Los Feliz and Silver Lake on the Los Angeles Basin side and the equestrian neighborhoods of Burbank and Glendale on the San Fernando Valley side, Griffith Park is a retreat from the urban, their very own section of the Santa Monicas. What they experience is an altered and sometimes enhanced version of the mountains. Fed by a natural spring and landscaped with boulders from other sections of the park, Fern Dell just north of Los Feliz Boulevard is one of the more beautiful of the quasi-natural spots in the range. While Fern Dell is the commonly used name, the area was originally known as Mococahuenga Canyon and once served as a gathering place for Tongva Indians in the area. Ferns native to the Santa Monicas and an assortment of imported species grow along a trickling stream. Shaded by native sycamores and alders, as well as planted coast redwoods growing significantly farther south than their current natural range at the lower end of Big Sur, this glen on the edge of Hollywood has the feel of a temperate rainforest. Its lushness contrasts sharply with the brushy and perilous slopes that most people associate with the park.

While there are numerous large groves of imported eucalyptus, the park still has a good representative sampling of native Santa Monica Mountains vegetation. Stands of chaparral and coastal sage scrub cover the steep slopes and park trails head out into woodlands where coast live oak and black walnut grow. In spots, there's a nice mountain tableau where the famous Hollywood Sign stands in the background behind some toyon, a small chaparral tree that is commonly known as California holly. Many accounts even credit this plant

Chaparral and Skyscrapers: Just six miles beyond a Griffith Park hillside thick with chaparral, downtown Los Angeles glowers under a stormy winter sky.

with giving Hollywood its name. The fact, however, is that the toyon is not a true holly, nor are these stories accurate.

Hollywood, once a small farming community independent from Los Angeles, got its name after the wife of founder Horace H. Wilcox heard it while traveling back east. Then, as so many things have been, the name was imported to California. In keeping with the spirit, if not the biology of the moniker, Mr. Wilcox tried planting some actual holly bushes in Hollywood but they died.

The Hollywood name, however, famously lives on, as do the toyon, if with less renown up in the hills. Toyon nearly had its own day during efforts in the 1970s to gain national park status for the Santa Monicas.

While the Toyon National Urban Park did eventually come into existence in 1978, it did so under the less evocative if more geographically inclusive name of Santa Monica Mountains National Recreation Area. There is, however, a Toyon Canyon Landfill in Griffith Park, which happened to be where the mountain lion was first spotted.

Place-name claims to fame notwithstanding, the toyon is one of the most appealing of the range's plants. A harbinger of the coming winter, usually in December, the toyon's clusters of berries ripen to a vivid red that stands out against its deep green, toothed leaves. "Here and there over the hills are brilliant patches—as though a generous hand wielding a great brush had trembled with the joy of his work and splashed his

Icons of Hollywood Hills: Corner of Frank Lloyd Wright's Hollyhock House shows architectural detail and frames a distant Hollywood Sign, with the Griffith Observatory on the right.

field with red," wrote John Russell McCarthy in the 1925 *These Waiting Hills*, one of the few books dedicated to the Santa Monicas.

The combination of colors and the berries' ripening near the holidays earned toyon another nickname: California Christmas berry. While laws restricting berry gathering were passed in the 1920s, Southern Californians have long ventured up into the mountains to harvest toyon berries for Christmas decorations. "How dear this cheerful little tree is to Californians . . . ," wrote Charles Francis Saunders in his 1923 book *The Southern Sierras of California*. "It is, indeed, a prime feature of the season, not to be omitted, though the stars fall. Anxious folk deplore the annual rifling of the bushes in the hills as surely leading to the plant's extermination; and indeed a sad amount of ruthlessness attends the business."

Ruthlessness has all too often found a home in Griffith Park. The park has a paradoxical reputation as both a sanctuary from the city and as a place where urban ills find a refuge on the edge of the wild. For all its beauty, there's a generalized sense of danger about the park, based mostly on legend, both historic and the contemporary urban variety.

The park honors the redundantly named Col. Griffith J. Griffith, who donated thirty-five hundred acres of the onetime *Rancho Los Feliz* to the city in 1896. A crowd gathered at City Hall to hear the mayor read a proclamation from Griffith announcing his Christmas gift to Los Angeles:

> The park will include some of the most romantic scenery of any park in the world. Not only will it be the largest park in the world, but its diversity of picturesque valley, hill, river and

mountain with its many varieties of trees and its rich undergrowth render it susceptible of being cultivated into the most beautiful of parks.

Griffith, too, was not without his contradictions: an early advocate for the social benefits of open space and parkland, he also went to San Quentin for the attempted murder of his wife at a Santa Monica hotel. His plea was alcoholic insanity, but neither the judge nor ultimately the public were mollified. Griffith Peak was renamed Mount Hollywood (the park's tallest at 1,625 feet) and the city refused a seven-hundred-thousand-dollar bequest made by Griffith following his release, although it did accept the money after his death in 1919. Some of those funds were eventually used for the construction of the Griffith Observatory.

The sense of unease about this section of the Santa Monicas reaches far back in city history and predates the park's establishment. A curse was supposedly placed on the land during the rancho era. The tale was made famous by California chronicler Horace Bell in his book *On the Old West Coast* and is now kept alive on the Internet. Bell, not one prone to subdued language, described the *Rancho Feliz* as, "the loveliest and most romantic property in Southern California, unexcelled, I verily believe, anywhere in the universe."

When Don Pedro Feliz died in 1863, his teenage niece Petranilla (who in some accounts is blind) received nothing in his will and the rancho instead came under the control of Antonio Coronel, a onetime mayor of Los Angeles. Petranilla then delivered a highly specific, *Californio*/biblical curse on the land: flood, fire, withering grapevines and violent death.

In Bell's account, she declared,

> A blight shall fall upon the face of this terrestrial paradise, the cattle shall no longer fatten but sicken on its pastures, the fields shall no longer respond to the toil of the tiller, the grand oaks shall wither and die! The wrath of heaven and the vengeance of hell shall fall upon this place . . .

And indeed many a bad thing did soon come to pass on the rancho, as they did throughout Southern California when the devastating drought of the 1860s decimated the region's cattle business. For that matter the fires and floods that occasionally swept the rancho seem more natural than supernatural in the Santa Monicas, while the violent deaths of some of those associated with the ranch were hardly out of the ordinary in frontier Los Angeles.

Bell goes so far as to claim that the curse motivated Griffith's decision to donate the land to the city. He even recreates a dialog between Griffith and his secretary that seems to anticipate the city's later desperation for parkland and its reputation for disaster. The distraught colonel laments what to do with the cursed land.

> Who in hell would take it—a place that is all taxes, no income and stocked with demons?

"Donate it to the City of Los Angeles!" cries the secretary, an inspired look in his eyes.

In more recent times, Griffith Park has gained notoriety thanks to the books of such neo-noir writers as Walter Mosley, James Ellroy and Michael Connelly as a dumping ground for bodies. The park offers both proximity and remoteness for such activity, and though at best sporadic in frequency, these incidents have become entrenched in the Southern California psyche.

For all the menace associated with the park, its most tragic event is all but forgotten. In October 1933, a welfare relief crew of more than thirty-seven hundred unemployed men earning forty cents an hour was clearing brush and working on a road project in the park. Temperatures climbed to one hundred degrees, and then a fire broke out in narrow Mineral Wells Canyon. Although none of them had firefighting training, the men went into the canyon with their shovels to fight what appeared to be a modest fire. The question remains whether a foreman ordered the men into the canyon and threatened to revoke work permits if the crew refused. But the resulting scene was a disaster.

An experienced fire warden, sensing the potential for catastrophe, ordered some of the crew out of the canyon. As they worked their way up the narrow paths, the workers encountered more men heading in to fight the fire. Then the winds picked up and shifted direction and flames began to overtake the workers.

Most managed to escape but others attempted to run directly away from the fire only to encounter steep slopes that slowed their flight. An eyewitness account described a horrifying sequence of death:

> You could tell the progress of the fire by the screams. The flames would catch a man and his screams would reach an awful pitch. Then there would be an awful silence. Then you would hear somebody scream and then it would be silent again.

The fire burned fewer than fifty acres but the official death toll was twenty-nine and some early estimates put the dead at fifty-eight men. Either figure would make it the largest loss of firefighter lives between the massive 1910 wildfires in the Northern Rockies and the September 11, 2001, attack on the World Trade Center. A small tribute to the victims disappeared long ago. For decades the incident went uncommemorated until 2004 when a new memorial was finally dedicated in the park.

Perhaps because of its location in the middle of the city, Griffith Park has long been subjected to attempts to improve the land or seize it for other purposes. In 1957, a 2.7-mile stretch of the Golden State Freeway along the west bank of the Los Angeles River opened on what had been two hundred sixty acres of parkland. During the 1960s and 1970s, the city proposed ambitious improvements for Griffith Park. The 1968 park master plan discussed construction of fifty helicopter pads and even an irrigation system to support artificial rainforests. The 2005 park master plan draft also advocated new development in the park including a pair of aerial tramways that drew strong negative reactions from local homeowners associations as well as the Sierra Club.

Balancing such pressures is a longstanding recognition that maybe, just maybe, the park's greatest worth is as open space and semi-wilderness for a region where hyper-growth has long been the rule. In 1911, the same year that five thousand rainbow trout were released into the river on the park's north end, the acting superintendent Frank Shearer declared,

> As Griffith Park will in the near future be a fair sample of Southern California's mountain scenery, easy of access to the visitor and resident alike, it would be a mistake to change the landscape effect by introducing alien features in the way of tree planting, etc. The native collection of trees and shrubbery which exists under present climatic conditions can be greatly enhanced by the proper methods of sylviculture and the introduction of an adequate supply of water.

(Native plants notwithstanding, Shearer was later instrumental in the creation of Fern Dell.)

The landmark 1930 *Olmsted-Bartholomew Plan for the Los Angeles Region* concluded,

> There is an enormous value to the people at large in a simple, quiet, beautiful open space screened in and kept free from all evidences of commercial activities and from the less attractive conditions of the outside world. This value can be created and developed only in such an area as Griffith Park . . .

High above Hollywood, Mulholland Drive, one of the most celebrated mountain roads in the world begins as an unmarked dirt walking trail in Griffith Park. The fifty-five-mile-long route that runs along the high ridgelines of the Santa Monicas and out to the Pacific is commonly described as beginning just west of U.S. 101 at the Cahuenga Pass. But east of the freeway and not even connected to the remainder of Mulholland, this brief stretch, an afterthought of the original road, extends eastward into Griffith Park. Bush sunflowers bloom above the road cut on slopes so crumbly that a California towhee foraging in the brush sends down micro-landslides of sand and pebbles. Beneath the road, a chaparral-cloaked canyon runs down to a drainage marked by sycamores with high green, new spring leaves standing out against the dark backdrop of brush. The chaparral is speckled in places by the pale pink florets on laurel sumac, a tree-like shrub that is one of the mountains' most prominent plants.

Mulholland Sunrise: Seen from a Mulholland Drive overlook above Cahuenga Pass, downtown twinkles and the Hollywood Freeway streaks into action as dawn comes to Los Angeles.

The road winds below the crest of the mountains for less than two miles, below the Hollywood Sign and the forest of communications towers atop Mount Lee—a site originally flattened in the 1920s to build a dream house for silent-film giant Mack Sennett. Whatever his penchant for comedy, Sennett also had a grandiose streak. For his three-hundred-four-acre "private mountain," he hired architect John De Lario to create a grand estate of granite and marble, hanging gardens and waterfalls that Sennett hoped would be visible for miles—"the greatest monument in the world," as he put it.

"I'll build an elevator," Sennett told friends. "An elevator that goes zoop, right up the mountain! And a swimming pool. And everybody who goes by will point

and say, 'That's where Mack Sennett lives.'" But that vision, like Sennett's Keystone Kops-built fortune and empire, fell to moviegoers' changing tastes and the onset of the Great Depression.

Beyond Mount Lee, the road passes a neighborhood of homes clinging to the slopes and disappears into a tangle of winding streets. Like the Los Angeles River, Mulholland Drive begins not with a bang but a trickle.

The Griffith Park stretch was planned as an add-on to the original Mulholland Drive that quite literally began with a trickle as its namesake William Mulholland christened the route's first section with water from the Los Angeles Aqueduct.

The dedication of the Mulholland High Way on

Mulholland Walnut: Along a serpentine stretch of Mulholland Highway, leaves on a native black walnut tree begin to turn.

December 27, 1924, brought together the Old West, Old California and modern California at a fiesta attended by fifty thousand people. The original road ran twenty-four miles from Hollywood to Calabasas, where a rodeo staged by silent-film star Tom Mix featured the western actor in a display of shooting. The *Los Angeles Times* noted that cowboys roped wild steers before stunt flyers took to the skies in an aerial circus.

> Two brilliantly caprisoned Spanish caballeros, mounted, stood guard at the gate. On the ground was the silken pillow on which the golden key to open the gates had been placed. Chief of Police Heath took up the golden key and presented it to Mr. Mulholland. The latter smashed a bottle of Los

Angeles Aqueduct water over the key and then inserted it into the gold lock holding the flowery chain together. The chain fell apart and the thousands of men, women and children assembled at the spot to witness the ceremony broke into a deafening cheer.

Then, trailing the limousines of Mulholland and his fellow dignitaries, the crowd piled into their Model Ts and set out east, across the new trans-mountain road in a motorcade to the Hollywood Bowl. There, speeches hailed the road and Mulholland himself. Lauded by one speaker as "The Empire Builder," Mulholland was modest in his remarks:

> I am glad to be here and wish to

demur myself against naming this drive after myself. I had little to do with it, but men of my acquaintance, men who have worked with me and who got most of their practical education on the aqueduct, did build it.

Indeed, the construction of Mulholland Drive represented a perpetuation of the water project's engineering imperative, and its convergence with real estate interests that sought to expand the growing city into their property in the wild hills above Hollywood. Automobile Club of Southern California historian Matthew W. Roth wrote of the engineers, "To them the road was its own justification: an artery, a vantage point, the technological transformation of nature to a sublime engineered landscape, and a monument to the revered forefather."

The completion of Mulholland's audacious Los Angeles Aqueduct had already reshaped several watersheds of the mountains. Filled in 1916, the two reservoirs in Franklin Canyon were used for storage and distribution for water transported from the Owens Valley via the aqueduct. Mulholland Dam was completed in 1924 and created the ninety-acre Lake Hollywood in the hills east of Cahuenga Pass. The curving Mission-style dam with its balustrades, arched façade and bear-head gargoyles transcends functionality and reflects the romantic, if not religious, symbolism of water in Los Angeles.

Despite the hopes and ambitions of the mountain real estate boosters, residential development in the Mulholland corridor lagged for many years behind the road's completion. But as building took place in the range, the ridges and folds of the Santa Monicas helped create discrete enclaves, sort of urban microclimates, where over the years distinct cultures evolved in various Hollywood Hills neighborhoods.

The most celebrated of those Hollywood Hills neighborhoods predates the highway. It sits along the western edge of Griffith Park, barely connected to Mulholland by a labyrinth of sinuous roads that seem better suited to a Mediterranean hill town than the automobile capital of the world. These days the neighborhood is often referred to as Beachwood Canyon but its true name is Hollywoodland, the development that the landmark Hollywood Sign was built to promote. Eighty years after its construction, the neighborhood has evolved into a prime example of the quintessential Southern California architectural and historic pastiche: the authentically inauthentic.

Dating back to 1923, Beachwood Canyon fea-

Two Sides of Mulholland: Near its terminus at Pacific Coast Highway, serpentine Mulholland Highway winds into mountains.

You've Been Warned: Signs along Mulholland reflect the clash between wilderness and the urban in many parts of the range.

tures a variety of historical revival styles, many created by its lead architect John De Lario working in a far more restrained manner than he had for Sennett. It's the kind of architectural mix that many people love about Southern California but that others see as evidence of the lack of a true regional style and as a theatrical attempt on the part of homeowners to claim an Old World heritage for themselves; farther west in the Hollywood Hills, Bel-Air literally had a coat of arms, with a shield showing a castle topped by a knight's helmet.

With set designers moving from the movies to residential architecture, Southern California design in the 1920s was heavily influenced by filmland fantasy. Architect Richard Neutra, who designed the Lovell Health House above Los Feliz and some of Southern California's most notable modernist homes, said the movies created a jarring eclecticism that resulted in "half-timber English peasant cottages, French Provincial and 'mission bell' type adobes, Arabian minarets, Georgian mansions on fifty-by-one-hundred-twenty-foot lots with 'Mexican Ranchos' adjoining them on sites of the same size."

Frank Lloyd Wright, whose arrival in Los Angeles helped bring Neutra and Rudolph Schindler to Southern California, was even more dismissive: "All was flatulent or fraudulent with a cheap opulence. Tawdry Spanish medievalism was now rampant."

There was nothing tawdry about Hollywoodland but it certainly reached back to an idealized Spanish past. Compared to some Los Angeles neighborhoods, it had far fewer wild design swings, although it had its touches. Residents entered through a pair of Gothic gates created by Old World stonemasons and walked along granite staircases that connected narrow streets built on different levels of the steep hillsides. Just inside the gates, the Hollywoodland Tract Office was housed in a Tudor-style building, which of course sat next to a Spanish Colonial Revival house. Mixed throughout the development were French chateaus, English cottages and Norman castles.

While hardly architecturally pure, Hollywoodland has aged beautifully and evokes Old Hollywood if not necessarily Old Spain. Over the years it has been home to a surprising range of characters, among them Hollywood's Busby Berkeley and mobster Bugsy Siegel, whose house was later bought by the singer Madonna.

Novelist James M. Cain lived in the neighborhood and set the beginning of his classic *Double Indemnity* in the canyon. He wrote of a "House of Death" with blood-red velvet drapes and a Mexican rug, that is, one made in Oakland.

> It was just a Spanish house, like all the rest of them in California, with white walls, red tile roof and patio out to one side. It was built cock-eyed. The garage was under the house, the first floor was over that, and the rest of it was spilled up the hill any way they could get it in.

Hollywoodland was by no means the most exclusive community in the Hollywood Hills. Whitley Heights dates back to the end of World War I and its residents included leading silent-film stars, most notably Rudolph Valentino. Less vertiginous and with grander, more traditional estate properties, Laughlin Park, just south of Griffith Park in the Los Feliz district, was also a popular neighborhood in the early days of the industry, with residents including Charlie Chaplin and Cecil B. De Mille (who moved there from a rustic cabin in Cahuenga Pass).

Up until the 1920s, settlement in the mountains had been largely limited to such cabins and scattered homesteads. But advances in earthmoving equipment, increased mobility thanks to the growing popularity of automobiles, and the city's burgeoning population led developers to turn increasingly to the mountains for homesites.

In his autobiography, Wright, who was then enmeshed in construction of the Hollyhock House for oil heiress Aline Barnsdall near the base of the Santa Monicas, recalled the building boom in the mountains. "There the Anglicans (sic) were busy as could be with steam shovels tearing down the hills to get to the top in order to blot out the top with a house in some queasy fashionable 'style,' some esthetic inanity or other."

Hollywoodland's developers, which included Harry Chandler of the *Los Angeles Times*, touted the transformation of the canyon from near-wilderness to residential district. But like today's developers in the Santa Monicas, they used the mountains as a selling point, celebrating Hollywoodland's proximity to the

International Icon: From its perch along the slopes of Mount Lee, L.A.'s most famous symbol, the Hollywood Sign, looms over palm-lined Beachwood Drive.

increasingly vulnerable "everlasting hills."

"Live where art and science are in accord with nature," read one early advertisement, while another touted how "the effectiveness of architectural beauty is enhanced by the friendly boughs of the ancient oaks." Residents were shown riding through the chaparral on horseback and at lushly landscaped homes where exotic plantings prospered under ideal growing conditions.

So, too, apparently would children. "Husky limbs and lusty lungs for the kiddies of the hills," read one description. In another tribute, a Hollywoodland resident, Dorothy Davis Conant, wrote of going to the doctor and seeing children from the city's flatlands being administered sun-ray treatments after a particularly foggy and rainy winter. With the other mothers looking on admiringly, she then "pointed to the sun-browned skin of my boys. There had been enough sunshine to

make them the color of little Indians."

As is so often the case in the Santa Monicas, nature eventually exacts a price for all that sweet air and sunshine. Back in 1956, the canyon's commercial village had provided the setting for a scene of panic and flight in the original *Invasion of the Body Snatchers*. On the night of May 12, 1961, it was not pod people but wildfire that forced an evacuation of the canyon as winds gusting to sixty-seven miles per hour snapped a power line, then sent the ensuing fire through the brush and neighborhood.

The fire eventually reached the home of *Brave New World* author Aldous Huxley, who had settled in the canyon in 1956 after a peripatetic spiritual and geographical journey through Southern California. The Santa Monicas made a few unbilled cameo appearances in Huxley's work. In his 1939 novel *After Many a*

Summer Dies the Swan, Huxley set the castle of a millionaire in the mountains above the west end of the San Fernando Valley. He wrote of the Southern California landscape as "a desiccated Scotland" and likened the up-and-down zigzags of the high mountain ridge to a stock market graph. And as his compatriot Evelyn Waugh later did in *The Loved One*, Huxley lampooned the excesses of Forest Lawn, the famed memorial park in Glendale with a Hollywood Hills location that climbs the north slope of the Santa Monicas above Burbank. Like many Europeans who settled in the mountains, Huxley compared the Santa Monicas to the Mediterranean. He described his Beachwood view as looking out "over completely savage hills . . . hills which remind me a little of Greece by their barrenness, their steep-sided narrow valleys and the unsullied sky overhead."

When the fire broke out, Huxley was working on the final chapter of his novel *Island*. He was able to save the draft although he did lose the personal letters, manuscripts and books he had amassed over a lifetime. In a typically surreal Southern California episode, he circumvented police roadblocks by riding with street gang members after saving his car and going to tank up in Hollywood as the fire raged.

His wife Laura Huxley beautifully captured the fragile balance of life in the mountains, even in the comparatively urbanized Hollywood Hills, where a single spark can transform paradise into hell in a matter of moments. She wrote that on the night of the fire,

> Everything was supernaturally clear. The immense city below extended all the way to the Pacific, shimmering with millions of lights. The outline of the hills behind our house was dramatically black against the clear dark blue sky. Everything had a limpid, shining quality of newness and eternity.

The fire destroyed eight homes and damaged nine others as it burned more than eight hundred acres. By Santa Monica Mountains fire standards it was minor, although its effects would be felt again months later. With the loss of so much vegetation, rains the following February sent four feet of mud and boulders cascading through the neighborhood.

Years before it was developed as a residential community, Beachwood Canyon played a major role in the genesis of one of Southern California's premier cultural institutions: the Hollywood Bowl.

Along a pathway at the Bowl, a plaque attached to a granite boulder celebrates a 1916 pageant-style production of *Julius Caesar* that took place in Beachwood Canyon's natural amphitheater. The play, which commemorated the three hundredth anniversary of Shakespeare's death, featured a literal cast of thousands, most notably Tyrone Power as Brutus and Douglas Fairbanks, Sr., in a smaller role. It was such a success that a group was later formed to establish a permanent open-air facility for similar productions. Daisy Dell, a site in the Cahuenga Pass that boasted outstanding natural acoustics, was then purchased by a group called the Theater Arts Alliance.

One of its leaders was Christine Wetherill Stevenson. She had already staged productions at Krotona, a Theosophical colony on a fifteen-acre parcel in Beachwood Canyon. Theosophy is a spiritual tradition that emphasizes the unity of all existence and universal law and the colonists at this site also believed that their land had a special spiritual power and was "magnetically impregnated." The mountains have long been the location for a variety of religious, utopian and communal sites and settlements. Stevenson, a Theosophist, and some others in the Alliance wanted to use Daisy Dell for religious productions, which led to a split and eventual dissolution of the group, as well as the evolution of the Hollywood Bowl into the summer home for the Los Angeles Philharmonic.

No one has ever proved that the Bowl was magnetically impregnated but those who convene on a warm summer night swear its magic is tangible. Even with the Hollywood Freeway coursing nearby and seating for eighteen thousand rising into the hills, the bowl evokes the amphitheaters of ancient Rome or Greece and successfully fuses the natural and the cultural. Some Hollywood Bowl-goers even claim they have heard coyotes harmonizing with the music. "The Chalice in the Hills," a poem by Warner Van Valkenburg featured in a 1926 program, celebrates this element of the Bowl experience:

And when the baton low is cast,
A mockingbird from yonder glade,
Nestling in a yucca tree,
Pipes a mocking melody—
And sings, and sings on, unafraid.

In his autobiography, conductor Bruno Walter wrote of its forested setting:

> It was uplifting indeed to conduct in that bowl while the orchestra strove devotedly and the many thousands filling the vast amphitheater way up into the mountains listened eagerly . . . There was the splendor of the California night, of the starry sky and of the dark mountains surrounding us; there was the touching silence of the immense throng . . . My musical conscience, stunned by so much beauty, yielded, and I became overcome by a mood of happy exultation.

Prime boxes at the Bowl are passed down through the generations. While they offer the best view of the stage, they miss the best part of the show. It's from the cheap seats that comes the full Bowl experience. In the distance, the flat ridge of Mount Lee and the Hollywood Sign rise above the nearer hills of the Cahuenga Pass. Behind the bandshell and climbing to Mulholland Drive, rounded golden hills, mottled by a mix of laurel sumac, coast live oaks and eucalyptus, redden in the low-angled light of sunset as the concert begins, before dimming and disappearing into the night. In his legendary 1934 production of *A Midsummer Night's Dream*, film and theater director Max Reinhardt incorporated the hills into his staging. The show starred Mickey Rooney as Puck and Olivia de Havilland as Hermia; it was during this production that she was discovered by Jack Warner.

Drawn by opportunities in the film industry, Reinhardt was among the first of the German artists and intellectuals who immigrated to Southern California. In the 1930s and 1940s, many leading European composers and conductors who had been driven to the United States by the rise of Adolf Hitler found a musical refuge in this canyon above Hollywood. Otto Klemperer, musical director of the Los Angeles Philharmonic, and Igor Stravinsky,

who lived in Southern California for nearly forty years, conducted at the Bowl, while twelve-tone scale innovator Arnold Schoenberg composed a special concerto for the venue. And in 1942, Vladimir Horowitz had "the greatest moment of my life" after Sergei Rachmaninoff appeared onstage to tell the pianist that his performance of Piano Concerto No. 3 was how the composer always dreamed the piece should be played.

Just as some of the twentieth century's most important classical music figures came to these hills, so too did leading Modernist architects. For all the periodic hazards that the Santa Monicas pose to residential development, its ravines and ridges have proven to be a unique, if irregular, architectural canvas.

Frank Lloyd Wright arrived in 1917 to work on the Olive Hill project for Aline Barnsdall, which she had envisioned as an avant-garde arts complex. The main building (which became known as Hollyhock House for the abstract floral motif that Wright incorporated) rose on the hill, a small knob with commanding views that sat near the base of the Santa Monicas in Hollywood. It would be a stretch to say that the complex that Wright designed is literally in the Santa Monicas, but the mountains seem to have influenced the site of the buildings. Wright's preliminary sketches show the house oriented against a distant ridgeline. The ridge is rendered with a single line but follows the general contour of the mountains that would ultimately form a backdrop for the buildings.

Wright's time in Los Angeles would prove to be one of the most significant stages of his career. It was here that he built his first textile block houses, which were constructed from both plain and patterned concrete blocks. Both in style and construction, these houses represented a significant departure from the Prairie School designs of Wright's early career. Three of the four were built in the Santa Monicas, and considering that Wright was committed to developing a native architecture for California that was in harmony with the region's terrain and climate, the Santa Monicas no doubt influenced his creative direction. He even talked about using the mountains' gravels in the mix from which the blocks would be made.

Built on the edge of Griffith Park, the 1924 Ennis House was the most monumental of the textile

Spring Green: A gnarled and twisting valley oak near the base of Boney Ridge leafs out with new green at Rancho Sierra Vista/Satwiwa.

block houses. Wright lauded it by telling its owners that a hundred years after its construction "pilgrimages will be made to it by lovers of the beautiful . . . " Though badly damaged in the 1994 Northridge Earthquake, it does in fact draw Wright's disciples and European tourists up a twisting Los Feliz road. Still, the house has its detractors, notably Wright biographer Brendan Gill, who wrote that the structure "threatens to crush the hilltop upon which it sprawls . . . "

As grand, if not overpowering, as it is, the Ennis House was hardly Wright's most ambitious design for the Santa Monicas. In 1923, he began making plans for a massive development on more than four hundred acres of

land on the Doheny Ranch, now part of the Trousdale Estates area of Beverly Hills. The tract belonged to oil magnate Edward L. Doheny, although there is no record that he was directly involved with the project.

Wright's design was more than pure speculation, however, and closely followed the topographical details of the land, although he referred to the mountains as the San Gabriels, not the Santa Monicas. That said, he clearly had an affinity for the range: "Curious tan-gold foothills rise from the tattooed sand-stretches to join slopes spotted as the leopard skin, with grease bush . . . " Doheny Ranch is a fantastic and exotic design with a dramatic arched span over one ravine, hanging gardens and houses that closely orient to the contours of the hills. One house features a cascade flowing beneath the house, formed by a fountain and runoff from the natural drainage, assuming that there has been any recent rain.

Gill says the design for Doheny Ranch was among the most grandiose and romantic of Wright's career. Doheny Ranch would never amount to anything other than a set of dreamy renderings, but it did influence other Wright projects. The Ennis House was based on one of the Doheny designs and the waterfall house anticipated the premise of one of Wright's masterpieces, Fallingwater in Pennsylvania.

During the late 1940s, Wright and his son Lloyd also developed elaborate plans for a resort hotel complex of cottages in Runyon Canyon. The only structure actually built was a Lloyd Wright-designed pool house where Errol Flynn lived. Frank Lloyd Wright's legacy in the Santa Monicas includes a pair of later structures, the 1939 Sturges House in Brentwood and the 1940 Oboler Gatehouse high above Malibu. But his historic role transcends his own designs.

While working on Hollyhock House, Wright was distracted by the ongoing construction of his design for the Imperial Hotel in Tokyo. Lloyd Wright, whose distinguished career included such designs in the mountains as the Samuels-Novarro House and two bandshell designs for the Hollywood Bowl, supervised construction for a time. Then in December 1920, Vienna native Rudolph Schindler, who had been working for Wright's Chicago office, arrived in Los Angeles to complete the job.

On their first full day in L.A., Schindler and his wife Pauline went to Olive Hill with Wright and were dismayed as they looked toward the Santa Monicas. The dry season was just ending following a year of below-average rainfall and the hills were at their desiccated worst. "As we looked toward the thirsty hillsides it was the fresh green of the Wisconsin landscape we longed for," wrote Pauline.

But Schindler quickly began to accept the Southern California landscape on its own terms, according to architectural critic Esther McCoy, who noted that "the brown tones brought out the shapes of the hills and satisfied Schindler's intense interest in form: their tawniness against the blue sky provided a new combination of colors for his palette."

Like Wright, Schindler sought to create architecture in synch with the landscape, aiming for work that was "as Californian as the Parthenon is Greek." He went on to become one of Southern California's most influential architects and built nearly a hundred fifty buildings in the region, many in the Santa Monicas. He's best known for his works in the hills above Silver Lake but also created a number of houses in the Hollywood Hills and on the San Fernando Valley side of the range above Studio City. Farther west in the hills that ring the Valley, he designed houses for the Park Moderne development in what is now Calabasas and his 1940 Van Dekker house in Woodland Hills nestled into rolling hills with a roofline that echoed the terrain.

Just as Wright had lured him to Los Angeles, part of Schindler's historic legacy derives from his role in drawing another legendary modern architect to the region.

In his early years in Los Angeles, Schindler maintained a correspondence with a fellow young architect from Vienna named Richard Neutra. Neutra, already intrigued by the possibility of working for Wright and fascinated by California, had his eyes set on America. He worked briefly for Wright in Chicago, then with Schindler's encouragement came to Los Angeles in 1925.

The two men collaborated on several projects, including a design for the League of Nations complex, and for a period Neutra and his wife Dione lived with the Schindlers in their landmark experimental home on Kings Road in West Hollywood. But they had a major falling out after Dr. Philip M. Lovell chose Neutra to plan a house on the edge of Griffith Park high up on Dundee Drive. Schindler had already designed the famed Lovell Beach House in Newport Beach and had even begun preliminary work on the Los Feliz house. But according to many accounts, he also had carried on an affair with Lovell's wife Lea; this may have stood in the way of future commissions.

With his strong emphasis on indoor-outdoor living, Neutra designed the house to incorporate features that would encourage the kind of lifestyle that Lovell, a so-called drugless practitioner, was advocating—a health regimen based on diet, exercise and nude sunbathing, among other precepts. Dubbed the Lovell Health House, it went on to become one of the twentieth century's most significant architectural landmarks and was the first house in the United States to employ a steel frame. (Bethlehem Steel gave a discount on materials but there were still significant cost overruns.)

Lovell opened the house to the public and its design was considered so revolutionary that on the first weekend fifteen thousand people came to see it. The challenging site, what Neutra had described as an "inclined piece of rugged nature," is integral to the house's architecture. The house perches on the steep slope and works its way down below the lip of the canyon and into the ravine, with views to the Pacific from huge windows and balconies suspended over the canyon.

The Santa Monicas went on to have one of the highest concentrations of landmark Modernist houses in the country; five of the twenty-one most significant Modernist houses in the country were in the range, according to a list compiled by *Town & Country* magazine. The mountains provided the setting for many of the landmark houses that were built as part of the *Arts and Architecture* magazine Case Study program. Initiated in 1945 by the magazine, the program selected prominent architectural offices to develop prototypes for innovative yet inexpensive designs for the anticipated postwar homebuilding boom. The emphasis was on designs that employed new materials and construction techniques, and over a span of twenty-three years, twenty-four houses were completed, roughly half in the Santa Monicas. These houses represented the continuation of a Southern California Modernist tradition that architectural critic David Gebhard wrote was as significant as any in the world, yet long overlooked:

> While Le Corbusier, Mies van der Rohe and Walter Gropius were in the process of establishing the International style as a style in Europe, R.M. Schindler and Richard J. Neutra were doing the same thing in southern California. Although the early work of Schindler and Neutra laid the foundation for California's brilliant architectural renaissance of the late 1930s, its reputation, in contrast to its European equivalent, was almost entirely local and regional.

One of the defining images of Los Angeles is a photo taken in 1959 by architectural photographer Julius Schulman of Case Study House #22, a house west of Laurel Canyon Boulevard designed by Pierre Koenig. It shows two women wearing flowing dresses and sitting in a glass-walled living room cantilevered out from a Hollywood Hills slope. Beneath the corner of the room, there's a glimpse of a rock outcropping and some barely discernable vegetation. Beyond these features, which in some prints of the photo come out as pure shadow, speckled lines of lights stretch to the horizon before fading into the mist of a distant marine haze.

Although shot from a lower elevation, Schulman's image is the best known variation of photographs most typically taken from viewpoints along Mulholland Drive that portray Los Angeles as a vast, orderly universe of lights spreading toward the infinite. As Jean Baudrillard described the view, "Mulholland Drive by night is an extraterrestrial's vantage point on earth or, conversely, an earth dweller's vantage point on the galactic metropolis."

There's another iconic house higher up in the mountains just off Mulholland Drive and a bit to the east of Laurel Canyon. The eight-sided structure balances atop a pedestal that rises from the precipitous hillside and the house looks for all the world like a flying saucer hovering above the chaparral. Designed by John Lautner, who like Schindler and Neutra worked for Frank Lloyd Wright, it's known as the Leonard J. Malin House but is more commonly referred to as the Chemosphere. Thanks to its appearance in such movies as *Diamonds Are Forever* and *Body Double*, it has come to symbolize Los Angeles as a city of the future, city of the space age.

These two houses provide a bridge between the European-based high art aspirations that found a home in the mountains before World War II and the better known postwar American pop culture imagery of the range, especially as one moves farther west through the Hollywood Hills. In the popular imagination, Mulholland is a road of make-out spots and midnight racing along a series of deadman's curves high over the city and valley—as close to flying as you'll ever get on four wheels. The concrete channels of the L.A. River are for drag racers. Mulholland is street racing with panache and no margin for error, Formula One on a highwire.

Stilt Houses: Seemingly precarious, houses sit upon stilts anchored deeply into steep slope off Coldwater Canyon Boulevard just below Mulholland.

It's also a symbol of status and celebrity: a house in the hills, if not quite as precious as a Malibu beach house, remains a potent emblem of rank in Southern California. Mulholland is the Maginot Line between pricey homes on the Valley side and the even more expensive homes on the range's south face; the road forms the northern boundary of the verdant community of Bel-Air, touted as "the aristocrat of suburban development" and designed for the emerging city elite in the early 1920s.

The canyon roads that lead up to Mulholland are filled with manors, chateaus, palazzos and country estates, and it's less surprising that there are people with this much money than that there are so many of them to begin with. Cars, money and celebrities: Mulholland Drive is all that and in the eponymous David Lynch film, it all comes together in the opening sequence when a starlet's limousine is rammed by some teenagers racing along this serpentine Thunder Road.

With the exception of scattered parcels of nat-ural vegetation and parkland, the Santa Monicas in Beverly Hills and Bel-Air have been reinvented as a botanical fantasyland. Here the mountains are less a natural habitat than a geologic superstructure for extravagant landscaping. Slender Italian cypress trees tower over yards where oleander and hibiscus from China accent property lines and provide a vegetative screen—that is, when high walls clad with vivid bougainvillea from Brazil are not already doing the job. Ponderosa pines line Coldwater Canyon Boulevard as it crosses from the San Fernando Valley and into Beverly Hills, and Moreton Bay figs from Australia send their massive root systems sprawling across thirsty lawns of Kentucky bluegrass.

Artist David Hockney is particularly adept at capturing the range's combination of artificial and nat-ural environments. In *Portrait of An Artist (Pool With Two Figures)*, the deck of the swimming pool ends abruptly in mid-air. From there, a line of non-native landscaping, most prominently a pair of Italian cypress,

Mule Deer: With most of their natural predators gone, mule deer prosper in the Santa Monicas and often feed off the landscaping of suburban backyards.

stands out against the deep green textured slopes of chaparral. In the distance a progression of featureless ridgelines grows fainter before fading into the sky. It's the kind of juxtaposition that plays out countless times across the range.

Two other Hockney works focus on roads in the Santa Monicas. Nichols Canyon is a Hollywood Hills neighborhood east of Laurel Canyon and in a namesake painting, Hockney portrays a serpentine road lined by a few palm trees and some whitewashed houses with red-tiled roofs. But the hillsides are a fantastic rainbow of colors, not unlike those of the wildflowers found in the range: lavender, gold, orange and blue. In the neo-cubist *Mulholland Drive: The Road to the Studio*, the road climbs crazily through the hills and twists around bends, with the street grid of the San Fernando Valley and the Los Angeles Basin where you might expect the sky. The colors here are fantastic, too, but there are all sorts of elements that anyone who has ever driven Mulholland would immediately recognize: round grass-covered hills, enormous electrical towers, tennis courts, swimming pools and the lines of ubiquitous Italian cypress.

Rising up the slopes below Mulholland, Beverly Hills is famed for its parkway trees, where a single species runs the full length of a street; only its sycamores and coast live oaks are native to the mountains. Almost without exception in the Santa Monicas, if a tree is tall and growing anywhere but alongside a creek, it has been imported.

In its natural state, the Beverly Hills area was comparatively lush by Southern California standards. The Portolá party remarked on the wild grapes and roses in the area and the original rancho was dubbed *Rodeo de las Aguas*, which translated as "gathering of the waters." The name referred to the wetlands that formed at the base of the mountains where runoff from Coldwater and Benedict canyons accumulated.

The rancho's first owners were a couple: Maria Rita, a woman of mixed African and Mexican heritage, and her husband Vicente Valdez. They built a compound near today's Sunset Boulevard but Vicente died in 1828, thus setting off the first known dispute between neighbors in Beverly Hills history. A cousin, Luciano Valdez, also had claims to the land and decided to make a play to take over the entire rancho. Establishing the basic parameters for hillside property battles for centuries to come, he built his new house directly in front of Maria Rita's, thus blocking her view. In 1844, the aggrieved widow appealed to a council at the Los Angeles pueblo, which sided with her and ordered Luciano from the land. She did, however, have to pay $17.50 to compensate Luciano for his house and its non-native peach tree. However, Maria Rita's troubles were not entirely over. In 1852, the rancho was the site of the last Indian raid in the Los Angeles area, when a band of Utah Indians attacked the property. Two years later Maria Rita moved to the comparatively urban and civilized pueblo of Los Angeles.

As late as the 1870s, a time when Los Angeles

was doubling in population to more than eleven thousand residents, the Santa Monicas near the growing community were wild enough to serve as a hideout for the famed *Californio* bandit Tiburcio Vasquez.

Vasquez has the distinction of being the first pop star in the history of the Hollywood Hills. To some he was a folk hero: Robin Hood, Zorro and Pancho Villa all wrapped in one. To others, he was a no-good, cattle-rustling, stagecoach-robbing, murdering bandit.

Vasquez hardly fit the outlaw profile. He was born in 1835 to a well-to-do family in Monterey, the capital of California during Mexican rule. An educated man, Vasquez was fluent in both English and Spanish and wrote eloquent letters in a florid hand. He rode a golden Palomino and sometimes donned a red-lined cape.

By most accounts, Vasquez bristled at the changes that came to California with the arrival of Americans lured west by the Gold Rush. He claimed to be fighting a war of liberation against an occupying force, and once declared, "I believe we were unjustly and wrongly deprived of the social rights that belonged to us . . . Given sixty thousand dollars I would be able to recruit enough arms and men to revolutionize Southern California."

The end of his desperado days came at an adobe near the mouth of Laurel Canyon. A local character, Georgias Caralambo, owned the hideout. Dubbed Greek George, he had once owned Runyon Canyon as well as the land where the Hollywood Bowl now stands; he paid five hundred dollars. (A native of Turkey, he arrived in the United States with a herd of camels imported for use by the U.S. Army in the desert.)

Vasquez was ambushed by an eight-man posse that included a *San Francisco Chronicle* newspaper reporter named George Beers. The wounded Vasquez was taken to downtown Los Angeles, and there his life took on a surreal quality that predates today's celebrity justice culture. A large crowd gathered to see his arrival and society women visited him in jail. He sold autographed pictures of himself, and a play titled *The Life of Vasquez* opened at the Merced Theater near today's Olvera Street—his offer to play himself was rejected. Eventually taken to Northern California for trial, he was sentenced to hang and the ladies of San Jose swooned in the courtroom.

The mountains' evolution from frontier to haven for the stars was a rapid one. When Douglas Fairbanks and Mary Pickford purchased the Beverly Hills property that came to be known as Pickfair in 1919, it was a six-room hunting lodge. A Hollywood art director initially turned it into a Tudor-style estate before noted Southern California architect Wallace Neff remodeled it into an English Regency estate complete with marble floors and the only private screening room outside the White House. Pickfair established the template for Beverly Hills celebrity excess for generations to come. Its grounds featured an Olympic-sized swimming pool with a sand beach in one section, tennis courts and canoe ponds in a mountain range without any natural lakes.

While Fairbanks and Pickford were urbane pioneers in Beverly Hills, other early film stars moved into more remote stretches of the mountains west of the heart of Hollywood. Settlements in Laurel Canyon remained scattered into the 1900s but the area began to draw new residents and visitors when the country's first trackless trolley was established. The cars used overhead wires and connected to a Pacific Electric trolley route that stopped at the canyon's mouth. From there, riders would travel at four miles per hour to the Lookout Inn, a newly subdivided area called Bungalow Land and a roadside tavern.

The tavern was to become a unique pop culture landmark, providing a link between the silent-film era and the canyon's days as a center for the 1960s counterculture—a direct line from Tom Mix to Frank Zappa. And typical of the cross-generational celebrity overlay in the Hollywood Hills, Jimi Hendrix is said to have lived in a Laurel Canyon house once owned by that Tasmanian devil Errol Flynn (who seemed to live just about everywhere in the mountains over the course of his wastrel days), and at other times by W.C. Fields and Bugsy Siegel.

Mix was among the early silent stars, including Clara Bow and Ramon Navarro, who moved into the canyon. Mix bought the log cabin-style building, which had a bowling alley in the basement, although he only lived there briefly before moving to grander quarters in Beverly Hills on the same street as Charlie Chaplin and one block from Pickfair.

Unlike Beverly Hills, Laurel Canyon held onto its rustic character even as the city of Los Angeles spread

Cold War Relic: Once one of sixteen anti-aircraft missile sites around Los Angeles, this facility at the beginning of Dirt Mulholland now offers panoramas for mountain visitors.

into the flats below and the main road through the canyon was upgraded to serve as a cross-mountain connector between the San Fernando Valley and the L.A. Basin. By the late 1950s, most of what were then considered buildable lots had houses on them that averaged about twenty years old. The canyon's steepness meant that there were still thick stands of brush and a feeling of living in nature, even though the Sunset Strip was just a few minutes down the hill. It was isolated enough that for twenty-two years the Air Force operated a top secret, one-hundred-thousand-square-foot movie studio in these hills. The Lookout Mountain Studio was home to the 1352nd Photographic Squadron, which produced six thousand five hundred films, many of them focused on atomic testing, which remained classified for nearly fifty years.

With the rise of the L.A. music scene in the 1960s, Laurel Canyon offered a quasi-back-to-nature lifestyle and an easy retreat from the city for many of the emerging stars, a kind of Haight-on-the-hill, all golden light and mellow sounds, an overgrown thicket sheltering country rockers and folkies. One measure of the canyon's prominence is that from 1968 to 1969 its name appeared in song or album titles by John Mayall, Van Dyke Parks and Jackie DeShannon. And, in 1970, Joni Mitchell released the seminal *Ladies of the Canyon*.

Predating Mitchell's forays into more complex jazz arrangements, the album epitomizes the singer-songwriter genre forever linked with the canyon. Tracks such as "Big Yellow Taxi," "Woodstock" and "The Circle Game" cemented the blond, straight-haired Mitchell as a kind of Hollywood Hills hippie high priestess. "Our House," her then-boyfriend Graham Nash's sing-song ode to their cabin on Lookout Mountain Road, certainly contributed to the sense that this is where the cool kids were hanging and loving. The house invariably found its way into profiles of Mitchell as a way to encapsulate the Laurel Canyon scene, such as this 1969 account from *Time*:

> She lives in a ramshackle house in Los Angeles's Laurel Canyon, with secondhand trappings—brown velvet rockers, black and yellow crocheted

throws, a giant antique wooden pig, an old piano, a doll, stained-glass windowpanes and a sewing machine on which she makes her own dresses.

Laurel Canyon was a virtual brand, geographic shorthand for a sensibility less about the politics of the era than a kind of anti-style lifestyle. For a measure of Laurel Canyon's cultural resonance, consider that Carole King's *Tapestry* spent 302 weeks on the charts, the best-selling album of its day. It was largely written in the canyon and represented the introspective sensibility so often associated with this period in Southern California's musical history.

Even so, Laurel Canyon and the Hollywood Hills were certainly as much about sex, drugs and rock-and-roll as they were about peace, love and understanding. Bad craziness co-existed with mellowness in the canyon and the Zappa/Mix cabin became the scene of wild parties with a changing cast of the rock aristocracy as well as kids from the San Fernando Valley trying to crash the scene. The weirdness got to be too much even for Zappa, who soon moved out, but the cabin's reputation was established and it remained a hangout until a fire destroyed it in 1981.

The appeal of Laurel Canyon to L.A.'s creative community certainly transcended its 1960s heyday. When a 1979 fire destroyed twenty-three homes in the area, the victims were a microcosm of the canyon's denizens: actors, several film directors, a club owner, an animator, members of the band Pure Prairie League and blues rocker John Mayall, who lost his three-story home known as "The Brain Damage Club." Porsches and Mercedes melted, a nineteenth-century pornography collection and an 1831 Goethe Bible went up in flames, and a fourteenth-century Buddha was lost, as was a Steinway piano, numerous guitars and a stereo system that its owner claimed sounded like the Hollywood Bowl.

Filmmaker Lisa Cholodenko's 2002 film *Laurel Canyon* took a look at the canyon scene a full generation later. She captured the diffused light and overgrown, feral quality of the landscape, the rows of mailboxes at the bottom of winding roads and such surviving landmarks as the Canyon Country Store, the onetime Jim Morrison hangout and still the site where Canyon resi-

dents materialize each year for a group photograph.

What isn't revealed in the film is how the surviving rustic character of the mountains, both in Laurel Canyon and other Hollywood Hills areas, is under assault. As real estate prices have escalated and new construction techniques make it possible to build on forty-five-degree slopes once considered too steep and unstable, out-of-scale and ostentatious homes with massive retaining walls and foundations are ripping away at the mountains. The resulting battles between neighbors and fights over grading and ridgeline ordinances hark back to early efforts to limit development in the range, which ultimately grew into the movement to save the Santa Monica Mountains.

In the winter of 1951-52, downtown Los Angeles received more than twenty-six inches of rain, roughly eleven inches above average—although average is an imprecise term considering that yearly recorded rainfall here has ranged all the way from 4.42 inches to 38.18 inches. Precipitation throughout the Santa Monicas is considerably higher than in the flats and a few higher elevation areas in the range average seventy-five percent more rain than downtown.

Statistics aside, the January storm born in the Gulf of Alaska was a beast. It blew into Southern California and pummeled the region for three days, announcing rather strongly that seven straight years of subpar rains were ending. The rains also followed an unprecedented and largely unregulated building boom in the mountains following World War II. With the sun-baked earth unable to absorb the water, runoff poured down hillsides and across piles of loose soil that had been dumped into ravines as the hills were leveled and cleared for houses. Lacking native vegetation to stabilize it, the now-drenched soil turned into mudslides that carried debris and flowed freely through neighborhoods and often right through houses.

Writer and college professor Richard G. Lillard was living on Quito Lane in Beverly Glen at the time and wrote in his memoir *My Urban Wilderness in the Hollywood Hills*,

> The banks of bulldozed dirt above me
> at the head of Toyon Gulch hung like
> pillows on the edges of unmade beds,
> sopped up water, trebled in weight,

Acropolis Now: "I don't want anyone to say, 'What have you done to this wonderful site?'" said Getty Center architect Richard Meier. Some hail it as a modernist masterpiece, others lament its remoteness.

trembled, slicked themselves with the inundating moisture, and then in a berserk slurry sludged faster and faster down the steep slope, pulling with them everything roots had penetrated, skinning the hillside alive.

Lillard and other outraged Beverly Glen residents came together and formed the group Residents of Beverly Glen, Inc. to push for increased protections for their neighborhood. The Beverly Glen group then joined with other community organizations in the mountains to form the Federation of Hillside and Canyon Associations. The organization was a key player in the passage of the city of Los Angeles's first grading ordinance, what Lillard called "mankind's first comprehensive set of regulations for cutting and filling . . . Machinery would have to be more respectful of geological nature, contractors would have to be more conscious of the law of gravity . . . " But Lillard also acknowledged that the ordinance, while a landmark, didn't address questions about preserving the mountains themselves.

A few miles west of Beverly Glen, Mulholland Drive reaches Sepulveda Pass. The pass, once a natural footpath through the mountains, was supersized into the 405 freeway starting in 1957 and is invariably the site of some of Southern California's worst traffic congestion. While Los Angeles has fewer bottlenecks than the San Francisco Bay Area, the Santa Monicas remain a significant barrier to traffic. The Pass functions like the Bay Area's bridges and offers one of the only direct routes through the mountains.

Sepulveda Pass near Mulholland Drive is a cultural nexus of sorts, home to several private schools, the University of Judaism and the Skirball Museum. Just to the south, Mount St. Mary's College is virtually hidden high in the hills while the Getty Center, designed by New York architect Richard Meier, commands a promontory with the power and assertiveness of a fortress. Vilified before it opened for its mountaintop remove from the city, The Getty, like the Griffith Observatory sixty years before it, takes full advantage of its location.

Mulholland awkwardly jogs over the freeway and continues on the west side of the Pass, running along

the Valley side of the ridge in Encino for about one-and-a-half miles. And then, the asphalt ends and Mulholland Drive, one of the most famous streets in a region where even the rivers are paved, amazingly turns to dirt. It was here that the movement to preserve the Santa Monica Mountains had one of its first major victories.

The nine-mile-long Dirt Mulholland could have given way to a four-lane trans-mountain highway and, almost certainly, to massive development in the mountains. A 1959 state freeway plan approved by the California Legislature had also called for the extension of the Antelope Valley Freeway through Topanga Canyon and other freeways through Malibu Canyon and the Hollywood Hills. And in the early 1960s the Sunset Seaway plan was unveiled. It would have created an eight-lane freeway along a causeway four thousand feet offshore between Santa Monica and Topanga Canyon, requiring nearly a hundred million yards of landfill that would have been hacked out of the mountains.

A grassroots coalition that combined affluent homeowners, in some cases more interested in their quality of life than ecology, and the growing environ-mental movement led by the Sierra Club fought the state plans. To raise awareness of the area, Jill Swift organized a series of hikes along Dirt Mulholland and other areas of the mountains. Those hikes were successful and modest in scale, until a well-promoted March on Mulholland was organized in 1971 and drew five thousand people.

Now the only major structure on Dirt Mulholland is the Cold War-era Nike missile site, where radar once scanned the skies for attacking Soviet bombers. The road heads west along the high ridge of the mountains. To the north, suburban sprawl extends across the San Fernando Valley and creeps up benches and drainages into the mountains. But to the south, the view looks across the vast stands of chaparral that comprise the collection of parkland dubbed the Big Wild. Unlike the surrounded areas further to the east, it doesn't feel like some remnant island of nature, and is, in fact, the largest open space in any American city.

This is where the hills end and the mountains begin.

The High Road: Fog drifts beneath a canopy of oaks and over a blanket of fallen leaves at this idyllic spot in Malibu Creek State Park.

Hillside Community: A pair of chaparral yucca sends their towers of creamy blossoms over a watercolor-like assemblage of mountain plants, including lupine and non-native mustard.

Mountain Leaves: While the Santa Monicas don't put on a New England-style fall display, its autumn color comes as a surprise to those who assume that Southern California has no seasons.

Offshore Vista: Viewed from Santa Cruz Island, serrated Boney Ridge can be seen on the far left as the Santa Monicas stretch east along the Malibu Coast.

Wave Rider: An egret stands atop a kelp bed in a cove at Leo Carrillo State Beach, one of the healthiest marine environments in Southern California.

Bare Oak: A valley oak in the southern end of Chesebro Canyon is seen in spring before the deciduous tree leafs out.

Millennial Morning: Seen from Castro Crest, fog fills the valleys and canyons of the Santa Monicas early on January 1, 2000.

Conejo Buckwheat: A state-listed rare species, this buckwheat survives in a few coastal sage scrub areas in the western Santa Monicas.

Above the Clouds: Bare sandstone outcrop looks almost desert-like as clouds drift through the valley beneath Castro Crest.

Rock Pool Sycamores: With leaves turned gold in late autumn, sycamores grow within the volcanic grotto of Malibu Creek State Park's Rock Pool.

Home on the Edge: Chaparral fills gaps between sandstone slabs on Saddle Peak beneath a house perched along the rim of a cliff.

Getty Villa: Inspired by the first century Villa dei Papiri, the Getty Villa first opened in the early 1970s, then underwent an extensive renovation and the addition of new buildings before reopening in 2006.

Eagle Rock: The most prominent of Topanga State Park's sandstone outcrops, this landmark offers panoramic views as well as several wind- and water-carved caverns.

Cold Creek Waterfall: Considered the purest stream in the Santa Monicas, Cold Creek flows year-round and eventually reaches Malibu Creek.

Details of a Range: From threatened plants, incuding a dudleya growing from a crevice in a rocky crag and Braunton's milk-vetch along a
scrub-covered hill, to a starfish in a wave-splashed tidepool, life finds
a way in the sometimes challenging habitats found in the mountains.

Craggy Bloom: Monkey flower and other plants find survival opportunities in the crevices and crannies of Castro Crest's sandstone.

Malibu Creek: Yellow and orange sycamore leaves are at their most brilliant as an early morning fog bank clears, as ghostly images of trees on the opposite shore reflect in Malibu Creek.

Dume View: Seen from atop Point Dume, waves roll onto Westward Beach. It stretches into Zuma Beach, with the western range dropping to the Pacific in the distance.

Water Sign: Sycamores have always been a reliable indicator of the presence of water. Especially in fall as their leaves turn, sycamores clearly outline the range's watercourses.

Suburban Edge: The value of open-space preservation is evident as Newbury Park bumps up against moor-like hills at the National Park Service's Rancho Sierra Vista/Satwiwa.

Twilight on Boney Head: In the high country of the western Santa Monicas above Rancho Sierra Vista/Satwiwa, the ridge's volcanic rock is painted red as dusk nears.

Ranching Legacy: Once part of the Morrison Ranch along lower Chesebro Creek, this house is a remnant of the range's long history of stock grazing.

Roosting Egret: The pristine white of a great egret stands out against the mountains' deep green vegetation. Its plumes were once coveted for fashion accessories.

Indian Paintbrush: Common throughout the Santa Monicas, the brilliant reds of Indian paintbrush make it one of the range's most striking wildflowers.

White Oak Barn: Massive, stalwart trunk of a centuries-old valley oak looms over a classic barn at this Las Virgenes Valley farm.

Valley Oak Savanna: Unlike coast live oaks, valley oaks are deciduous. By December they add a touch of autumn color in such areas as Cheeseboro Canyon.

Edge of the Range: Green with winter rains, the Santa Monicas slope toward the Pacific at Circle X ranch as storm clouds hover over the distant Channel Islands.

Candleflame Lichen: Yellow-green growth of candleflame lichen patinas fallen tree branches. The lichen also is often orange in color and is considered harmless to trees.

Breaking Storm: Sunlight pokes out beneath an offshore mammatus cloud. Infrequently seen in Southern California, these ominous-looking clouds appear after the worst of a storm passes.

eading west from downtown Los Angeles, the Santa Monica Freeway runs parallel for fifteen miles to the mountains that indirectly gave this section of Interstate 10 its name. The freeway's elevated perspective five miles south of the Santa Monicas shows the city's densely developed, gridded flats sloping up to the mountains, where the southern face is mottled by houses that climb nearly to the ridgeline.

The interstate is nearing the end of its nearly twenty-five-hundred-mile run that began in Jacksonville, Florida. The homestretch is choppy with frequent slowdowns and a final junction with the San Diego Freeway before the big payoff at the Pacific. But like the Colorado River trickling into the desert sands before reaching the Sea of Cortez, Interstate 10 (dubbed, if never actually referred to, as the Christopher Columbus Transcontinental Highway except in one song by the Continental Drifters) doesn't quite make it to the ocean.

Not far past a 1940s-vintage Sears store in Santa Monica, Interstate 10 unceremoniously morphs into California Highway 1, the Pacific Coast Highway. The highway disappears into the darkness of the McClure Tunnel, swings right and emerges into the bright sunshine of the California Dream.

PCH runs along the base of the Santa Monica Palisades, a fanglomerate or edge of an alluvial fan that marks the onetime reach of the Pacific. Bicyclists and in-line skaters sail down the South Bay Bicycle Path and sunbathers spread out on the broad sands. A turn of the head or a glimpse in the rearview mirror reveals a slowly rotating Ferris wheel atop the Santa Monica Pier, which juts out beyond the surf line.

Straight ahead and due west, the view is grander, almost brooding. The Santa Monica Mountains, lined up as a series of purple ridges that become progressively fainter as they extend toward the horizon, drop all the way down to the Pacific along the Malibu coast. The view may lack the pristine wildness of Big Sur but it is nevertheless impressive. For nearly thirty miles, the Santa Monicas are a coastal range, with a series of peaks rising two to three thousand feet within a few miles of

Hillside and Oceanfront: Pacific Palisades houses cluster on a steeply sloping face just above Pacific Coast Highway with the bluffs of Santa Monica in the distance.

Cheeseboro Bloom: Fiddleneck phacelia blooms in Cheeseboro Canyon, one of the earliest National Park Service acquisitions. It's part of the Malibu Creek watershed.

the ocean; the range's tallest mountain, Sandstone Peak, reaches 3,111 feet just four miles from the Pacific, a climb that compares favorably with the steepness of parts of the Big Sur coast.

The corner where the mountains, the Los Angeles Basin and the Pacific converge is one of the most distinctive enclaves in the Santa Monicas. Although Pacific Palisades and Santa Monica Canyon are obviously urbanized, the sprawling metropolitan area feels more at a remove here. Instead of being viewed across miles of the city as it is from the Hollywood Hills, the ocean just to the south feels close enough for a half-gainer. The northern view opens up not to the San Fernando Valley but to the chaparral-covered slopes and jagged high peaks of Topanga State Park.

A series of canyons west of the 405 freeway—Kenter, Sullivan, Mandeville and Rustic—cut the moun-

tain face and descend toward the ocean before emptying into Santa Monica Canyon. Rustic is actually longer and deeper, but by name it is Santa Monica Canyon that reaches the Pacific after a brief run of a few miles.

Santa Monica Canyon cuts through a gently sloping but thick alluvial layer of gravel and rock that accumulated after being eroded and washed down from the mountains. Once known as *Boca de Santa Monica* after the original Spanish rancho here, as early as the 1870s the sycamore-shaded canyon emerged as a popular summer retreat and camping ground where dances were held on weekends. In 1887, the California State Board of Forestry established the nation's first forestry station, which began raising eucalyptus and other non-native trees in the hills of Rustic Canyon.

By the turn of the century, the canyon mouth had gained a reputation for its saloons, whorehouses and

Point Dume Headlands: Wave spray splashes onto the volcanic rock at Point Dume, which is the northwest boundary of Santa Monica Bay.

dance halls. But plans to establish the Port of Los Angeles just to the north never came to pass. So other than scattered buildings and silent-film director Thomas Ince's Inceville shooting location at nearby Santa Ynez Canyon, this corner of the mountains remained largely un-urbanized and remote from the city through World War I.

Over the next thirty years, however, Rustic and Santa Monica canyons and areas of the Pacific Palisades experienced a series of cultural episodes as an eclectic assortment of individuals and groups settled here, at least for a time. The Uplifters Club, well-to-do men affiliated with the Los Angeles Athletic Club, bought land in Rustic Canyon that was once part of the forestry station, and built a clubhouse and cabins for members. In their isolated, wooded retreat, the group reveled and put on often drunken productions, which included songs penned by early member L. Frank Baum, author of the *Oz* series.

A few miles farther up Rustic Canyon, the mountains remained secluded enough into the 1940s to draw a group of Nazi survivalists. In 1933, a parcel of land known as the Murphy Ranch turned into a Nazi enclave, designed to shelter a select community of believers who would emerge following a German takeover of the United States. Huge orchards were planted and a power station better suited to a small town was constructed. But the plan quickly unraveled not long after the attack on Pearl Harbor when authorities discovered the German national who had first convinced a local couple to buy and improve the property was a Nazi spy who had been communicating with the Fatherland via shortwave radio.

After the war, the same ranch went from Nazi haven to artists' utopia when grocery heir Huntington Hartford, he of the Runyon Canyon estate, bought it and

Dawn's Veil: Looking like an island archipelago, mountain peaks rise above fog formed as the sun slowly evaporates ground moisture following a winter storm.

established an artists' colony on this property and an adjacent parcel he purchased known as Camp Josepho. (A Russian-Jewish refugee named Anatole Josepho, who made his fortune in America after inventing coin-operated photo booths, had owned it.) Hartford brought in Lloyd Wright to design rustic studios and remodel existing structures on the 154-acre property. He granted fellowships to students and also brought in established artists. Painter Edward Hopper, poet Mark Van Doren and Austrian émigré composer Ernst Toch were among those who were in residence during the colony's fifteen years of operation.

Faced with mounting financial pressures and with speculation that the property would become part of the proposed Topanga State Park, in 1965 Hartford closed the colony and sold the land. The hope was that the state would continue to operate the retreat but a few months later Hartford sold the property to a private party. Among the final artists in residence was a nun

named Sister Gladys Ann, a twenty-year member of the order of Sisters of Loretto. Hipper than your average nun, she drove from the canyon to mass on Sunset Boulevard in a Thunderbird loaned to her by Jewish friends in Beverly Hills. While at the colony, she worked on such non-traditional works as a bronze of a skiing nun and the Marcel Duchamps-inspired "Nuns Descending the Stairs." As she explained to the *Los Angeles Times* about her order, "We are quite avant-garde, you know."

While the areas atop the mesas were pre-planned in the 1920s as affluent neighborhoods of Mediterranean architecture (one literally called California Riviera), the lower sections of Santa Monica and Rustic canyons evolved more organically into a rustic alternative. Its mix included the Uplifters' log cabins, beach cottages and Craftsman bungalows all set beneath towering sycamores and twisting coast live oaks along what was then a free-flowing creek. The area gained a reputation

as an artists' haven with a collection of Hollywood types, painters and writers. Photographer Edward Weston, who early in his career shot in Griffith Park, moved to the canyon and opened a studio here in 1935.

Writer Christopher Isherwood arrived in Santa Monica Canyon in 1939 as war came to Europe and wrote of the denizens,

> Their utopian dream was of a subtropical English village with Montmartre manners: a Little Good Place where you could paint a bit, write a bit and drink lots. They saw themselves as rearguard individualists, making a last-ditch stand against the twentieth century.

Even as the Murphy Ranch Nazis planned for their takeover of the United States, Santa Monica Canyon and the Pacific Palisades did become an unlikely refuge from the worst of the twentieth century's hor-

rors, certainly for an esteemed group of German intellectuals fleeing Nazi Germany. Thanks largely to the film industry, a number of German artists had come to work in Hollywood starting in the 1920s. Already established in Southern California, they provided their countrymen both assistance in escaping (as well as help with finding work, especially in the movies) and an established community for the émigrés once they arrived. For that matter, many of the émigrés were already accustomed to taking holidays along the Mediterranean, particularly the French Riviera's Sanary-sur-Mer. So despite the distance of thousands of miles, the climate and terrain of Southern California offered a safe and oddly familiar Mediterranean alternative. In the process, this corner of the Santa Monicas became a kind of Weimar del Mar.

Key among Santa Monica Canyon's artists was Polish-born actress and writer Salka Viertel. She had moved to Southern California with her German playwright husband Berthold in 1928 and eventually settled in Santa Monica Canyon on Mabery Street. Salka wrote screenplays, including several for films that starred her close friend Greta Garbo, including *Anna Karenina* in 1935. In 1940, at nineteen, the Viertels' son, Peter, wrote *The Canyon*, a celebrated coming-of-age novel about life in this enclave. He portrayed the canyon not as a Bohemian haven but as a vulnerable slice of Old California where the beach was just a short distance away and the open hills invited explorations and horseback rides. At no point does Viertel ever mention the Santa Monicas by name but the novel's most dramatic episodes are familiar ones in the range: fire, flood and real estate speculation. The book ends with his reflection on the taming of the canyon: "The lights and the moon have no chance to be reflected by the creek and there are no stables and ponds to fish, but—that doesn't matter. It's silly to mention it again. The thing to do is not think about it."

In his 1964 novel *A Single Man*, Isherwood also wrote about the neutering of the canyon into a kind of postwar seaside suburb. He wrote of signs warning not to eat the creek's watercress and the hordes of children who descended on the canyon as World War II veterans and their families discovered the area. "So, one by one, the cottages which used to reek of bathtub gin and reverberate with the poetry of Hart Crane have fallen to the occupying army of Coke-drinking television watchers."

Anacapa Island: An ominous sky hangs over the silhouetted profile of craggy Anacapa Island, second smallest of the Channel Islands.

Piuma Road View: South-facing perspective looks down upon Malibu Lagoon and Surfrider Beach and out over Santa Monica Bay to Santa Catalina Island.

As more European artists and intellectuals arrived in Southern California, the Viertels' home emerged as a veritable salon for the émigré community. During these Sunday afternoon gatherings hosted by Salka (Berthold was rarely there), some of the most prominent European intellectuals who had come to Los Angeles mingled with leading Hollywood figures, including Charlie Chaplin. Pacific Palisades historian Betty Lou Young writes that on one occasion a guest arrived and found, "Arthur Rubinstein playing the piano, Greta Garbo lying on the sofa, Christopher Isherwood lounging in a chair and Bertolt Brecht wrestling pots and pans in the kitchen."

The Viertels' home was not the only gathering place for the tight-knit community of exiles. In 1941, Lion Feuchtwanger, a celebrated German-Jewish histor-ical novelist once nominated for the Nobel Prize for lit-erature, arrived in the Palisades. After being held in a concentration camp in occupied France, Feuchtwanger and his wife Marta made a dramatic escape by foot over the Pyrenees. In 1943, for just nine thousand dollars, they bought a castle-like, Spanish-style home high up on Paseo Miramar above Sunset Boulevard. The location was positively Olympian: remote from the city and high up a steep and winding road, it commanded huge views of Los Angeles and Santa Monica Bay. Feuchtwanger dubbed it Villa Aurora.

As the war progressed, the couple restored the property and its gardens and hosted dinners that fea-tured readings from Feuchtwanger's works-in-progress. Less Bohemian in spirit than the Viertels' gatherings, these events drew numerous notables including Chaplin and German playwright Brecht, who lived nearby in Santa Monica. Feuchtwanger had helped Brecht escape

Mountain Thoroughfare: Once envisioned as a freeway, Malibu Canyon Road is cut into the slopes of its namesake chasm and remains a major route through the mountains.

to the United States and eventually reach Los Angeles. Brecht could barely tolerate the city and called it a "metropolitan Tahiti."

The leading figure of the Palisades émigré scene was Nobel Prize-winning novelist Thomas Mann. He arrived in the United States in 1941 and, after living in two residences in the lower reaches of the mountains, moved into a house he had built on San Remo Drive in the Palisades. Regarded by many as the virtual German head-of-state in exile, he was a regular at the Feuchtwanger gatherings and also made appearances at the Viertels'.

Some accounts suggest that one reason Mann moved to Southern California was to work on a Hollywood-based novel. That work never came to be but while in the Palisades Mann did write one of his most celebrated books, *Doctor Faustus.* On many levels,

Southern California remained elusive for Mann. He spoke of the "serene Egyptian-like sky" but also noted a certain artificiality to the landscape. That said, Kevin Starr in *The Dream Endures: California Enters the 1940s* quotes Mann's daughter Monica as saying "that the odd elegance of that distant shore, with its almost intangible beauty and worldly barrenness" helped free Mann from tradition and take more daring approaches with his writing.

And his most immediate surroundings were the Santa Monica Mountains, where beyond his gardens of fruit and palm trees, Mann looked out across the chaparral-covered slopes to Catalina. Gesturing toward the Pacific during a 1948 interview conducted at his home, he celebrated the range's beauty. "Here you find everything—the perfect climate, the hills, the sea, the strong contrasting colors of sky, earth and water."

eyond the Palisades, Pacific Coast Highway runs between the beach and the base of crumbling slopes where mesa-edge homes occasionally come tumbling down to the road. In one stretch, the cliffs have undergone an extensive stabilization project that is attempting to tame the slopes with twenty-two hundred feet of zigzagging, reinforced retaining walls and even burlap-covered chain-link fences.

PCH creates a false divide in the Southern California psyche between the beach and the mountains. But they are in fact inseparable. Take off from Los Angeles International Airport on a flight to Hawaii and look down as the jet follows the coast due west and the highway is reduced to insignificance. It becomes clear that the highway and riprap seawalls are artificial and ultimately inconsequential barriers: the Santa Monicas meet the Pacific on the beaches of Malibu.

With twenty-nine creeks flowing into the Pacific, the mountains' coastal face is cut by many more drainages than the range's north slope. Although almost unnoticeable to drivers along PCH, creeks draining from the slopes of the Santa Monicas reach the Pacific at an average rate of more than one per mile. The coastal canyons are some of the Santa Monicas' most verdant areas, shaded and cool retreats that provide escape from the sun-baked, desert-like aspect that the mountains take on during the long dry season.

Just inland from PCH, Escondido Canyon shelters the range's tallest waterfall. The trail to the falls, such as it is, begins at a parking lot along the highway, and is little more than a worn footpath along the shoulder of a road. The scenery in this first stretch is less of the mountains and more of developed Malibu. Huge houses are situated to take full advantage of coastal views. And so the path passes a few balustraded monstrosities where sprinkler systems go full bore right after a spring rain, spraying into the road in mid-afternoon and sending wasted rivulets of water down toward the highway. An assortment of invasive species—castor bean, fennel and mustard—line the trail.

The trail travels beyond the newer development and reaches a horse ranch with ancient thickets of prickly pear and century plants. It then enters a forest of coast live oaks and sycamores where wildflowers are sprinkled in the scrub beside the trail: brilliant red Indian paintbrush, the yellow-orange blossoms of sticky monkey flower and the deep pink-to-lavender flowers evocatively named Farewell To Spring.

The creek cuts across the trail at several points before the falls come within earshot. Just after a rain, runoff works its way more than two thousand feet down in a few miles before cascading down the three-stepped falls. The falls are notable both for their cumulative hundred-fifty-foot height and thundering volume after storms. But such prime displays are ephemeral, and, usually Escondido Falls flows modestly down a rock face covered by a curtain of lime deposits, drizzling off a covering of ferns and mosses before reaching the creek.

Virtually the entire stretch of PCH along the base of the mountains is contained within the boundaries of one of Southern California's most legendary Spanish land grant ranches, *Rancho Topanga Malibu Sequit.* Narrow, never more than two-and-a-half miles wide but twenty-two miles long, the enormous 13,316-acre ranch was originally owned by Jose Bartolome Tapia, who first visited the mountains in 1776 with his family as part of the de Anza expedition. The expedition camped in Malibu Canyon and legend has it that young Tapia went off on his own and explored the area on horseback before the group departed. The canyon's beauty left a lasting impression and decades later Tapia requested title to the land from the military commander in Santa Barbara, which he received in 1805.

The ranch remained in family hands until it was sold in 1844 to a Frenchman, Leon Prudhomme, who had married Jose Tapia's granddaughter. There was considerable confusion over land claims in California as the state went from Mexican to American control. Because there was no documentation of the original Tapia grant, Prudhomme's ownership was rejected. He remained on the land but the dispute helped set the stage for the rancho's acquisition by prominent Los Angeles businessman Matthew (Don Mateo) Keller for just fourteen hundred dollars—about ten cents an acre.

In addition to running cattle, in 1880 Keller established five hundred acres of vineyards on the ran-

Canyon Cascade: Ferns line Three Falls on Big Sycamore Creek, a verdant spot that challenges preconceptions of the Santa Monicas as an arid, desert-like range.

Above Trancas: Waves roll onto Broad Beach and Zuma Beach while Point Dume and the distant Palos Verdes Peninsula frame the dramatic Santa Monica Bay.

Rock Pool: Malibu Creek winds through the volcanic Goat Buttes and forms this sycamore- and reed-lined mountain haven, once a popular filming location.

cho for wine production. Keller, whose first vineyards were near present-day downtown Los Angeles, pioneered the region's wine industry and helped introduce California wines to the East Coast, where he opened warehouse facilities in Philadelphia and New York. Although he had an impressive city home in Los Angeles and built a ranch house in Malibu Canyon, in 1865 Keller also constructed a cabin in secluded Solstice Canyon that is now considered the oldest structure still standing in the mountains.

In Keller's day, the narrow, V-shaped canyon was known as Sosto or Soston Canyon, names likely derived from Loxostoxni, the Chumash village there. Now under the National Park Service, it's laced with trails, including one named for Keller's old wine label, Rising Sun. The main road up the canyon parallels Solstice Creek, a perennial creek shaded by a mix of

coast live oaks, sycamores and thick stands of alder. The creek flows over a series of dams built in the late 1930s and early 1940s by the canyon's owner, Fred Roberts, who some accounts say was trying to preserve the steelhead run up Solstice which is estimated to be at least ten thousand years old. In actuality the dams sped the demise of the steelhead run here. The National Park Service is trying to improve spawning conditions on the lower two miles of the creek by removing check dams and other barriers.

The trail passes the old Keller cabin and then about one mile up-canyon comes to the remains of a later and more celebrated house owned by the Roberts family. Designed by noted African American architect Paul R. Williams, Tropical Terrace was a modern ranch house set within a combination of the canyon's natural vegetation and rich gardens of palm trees and bird of

Tranquil Canyon: Just up from the tumult of Pacific Coast Highway, a grove of coast live oaks offers a serene escape at the National Park Service's Solstice Canyon.

paradise. The upper creek flowing down from Castro Peak was diverted into a series of pools and watercourses accessed by bridges and stone walkways. Across the creek, Roberts and his wife Florence hired an artist and mason to build a replica of the Shrine of the Virgin Mary at Lourdes. Built into the canyon's rock, the grotto-like shrine was framed by cascades of water. When it was finally completed after a year, the shrine was blessed with water from Lourdes.

For all its natural and spiritual blessings, Solstice Canyon is also cursed by fire. Over a seventy-year period, eleven fires have burned through the canyon, including several during the 1950s. After additional near-misses, a 1982 fire ripped through the canyon and finally destroyed the Roberts' dream house. What remains is tropical landscaping and stone terraces that suggest some remote outpost that has been overtaken by jungle. But also mixed in is an assortment of postwar American detritus: a gas range, sections of kitchen flooring and a concrete bomb shelter. In the Santa Monicas, the American Century, given Santa Ana winds and a spark, was just so much kindling.

Rancho Topanga Malibu Sequit entered its most famous era in 1892 when Frederick Hastings Rindge, a wealthy Massachusetts businessman who had moved to California for health reasons, purchased it from Keller. For Rindge, the rancho represented far more than a business transaction. A deeply religious man, he wrote of the land in biblical terms in his memoir *Happy Days in Southern California*. In various passages he likened the Santa Monicas to the Holy Land, to Eden or to Paradise.

Day's End: Reds and golds of sunset color the ocean and sky near Sequit Point at Leo Carrillo State Beach along the Ventura and Los Angeles county line.

The terrain itself was so life-giving for Rindge that he made reference to its "Ponce de Leon air." Rindge's language could certainly be florid at times but his writing offers some of the earliest and keenest appreciation of the Santa Monicas from an environmental perspective. And he had a particular fondness for the coastal canyons:

> The loveliest place to my mind, is a wooded cañon which opens to the sea, offering the crystal waters of its limpid brook as a libation to the spirit of the ocean; an offering brought from the high mountains, which near by gaze downward with wonder at the ocean's vastness; while the sea looks upward in admiration of the sierra's heights.

One of Rindge's favorite spots was Zuma Canyon, the area that he called "Zumaland." Zuma Creek begins high in the mountains and cuts through some of the most rugged terrain in the mountains. Steep volcanic cliffs tower above the creek, a perennial stream that descends over a series of waterfalls and through a channel thick with boulders on its six-mile course to the ocean.

> Tis the fairest valley of all those that grace these wonderlands. High mesas rise on either side guarding this nature's shrine. Great mountain crags form its background, while around the vale groves of branching sycamores, like sentinels, stand.

> The trees a circle make about thy
> graciousness
> As halo round a holy countenance
> Seen in February sunlight who shall
> dare say any other little valley can
> compare with this?

More than a hundred years later, even on an overcast day, it's difficult to quarrel with his conclusion. Fog drifts in from the nearby ocean, dropping a scrim on the canyon, softening the light and obscuring the details of the coastal sage scrub and chaparral on the surround-

helps reveal the sycamores' mottled bark, a mix of near-blue grays, tans and the faintest hints of rose. The bark's pattern is echoed in the textures and hues of the cobbles piled up in the streambed.

The stream enters the plain from a narrows, where virgin's bower bursts like asterisks from the scrub. A pair of mallards flies into the narrows before settling with a splash into a pool just below an old dam. The encroaching fog sends a tendril of mist along the canyon floor, which moves through the branches and eventually transforms the riparian forest into a black-and-white world of soft-edged silhouettes.

Zuma Creek flows out of protected parkland and through a concrete channel before it empties into the Pacific near Point Dume. Point Dume, a two-hundred-foot-tall volcanic headland, forms the northwestern boundary of Santa Monica Bay. One of the most prominent landmarks on the Santa Monica Mountains' coast, the point was a ceremonial landmark for Chumash fishermen. Although it sounds similar to such nearby Chumash-derived place names such as Mugu and Zuma (which Rindge took to be short for Moctezuma), Point Dume was named for Padre Francisco Dumetz by English explorer George Vancouver. Dumetz had hosted the captain at Mission San Buenaventura and Vancouver returned the favor by misspelling Dumetz's name as

ing slopes. The canyon floor, with its masses of reeds, has an almost boggy quality in many sections but is also notable for its forest: sycamores, coast live oak and black walnut. In early spring, the trees come alive with new textures and colors. The deciduous black walnut sprout fresh, bright green leaves and catkins, which dangle from the branches like some kind of elongated ornament. The coast live oaks don't drop their leaves all at once but do change with the seasons, putting out their own yellowish clusters of blossoms in spring. Sycamores trace the creek bottom, their leaves only beginning to bud. The lack of foliage

Ridgeline Development: Calabasas homes are situated on the edge of a rise. Ordinances designed to control ridgeline building have proven to be one the most contentious issues in the Santa Monicas.

Windsurfing Haven: Breezy conditions at Leo Carrillo Beach have made it a major destination for windsurfers. The beach is named for the actor and open space advocate.

Dume. Rindge, as well as some old maps, refers to it as "Duma" and in recent times the original "Do-May" pronunciation has been shortened to an ominous sounding "Doom."

Point Dume is one of the true garden spots along the coast. In spring its slopes bloom with California poppies and giant coreopsis, a member of the sunflower family that grows naturally only along the narrow Santa Monica Mountains coastal strip from Point Dume west and on sections of the Central Coast, as well as out on the Channel Islands. Coreopsis is a curious plant. Each is as individual as a saguaro, so oddly twisted and weirdly endearing that some people call them "Dr. Seuss plants." During the summer these low shrubs die back to gnarled and tattered tufts of withered brown leaves that hang limply from bare branches and down along a leathery, treelike trunk. They look just plain sad, deader than dead. When winter rains come, however, the coreopsis fill out with clusters of fingery leaves, freshly green and rubbery. Especially in February and March, they burst into bloom with clumps of vividly yellow daisy-like flowers.

Atop the point, the mountains' dual desert and marine character is revealed. This is, after all, a place where within a few minutes after spotting a roadrunner foraging in the coastal bluff scrub habitat, a pair of gray whales surfaces just off the point. It sounds beautiful too: surf, sea lions and the gamelan-like gong of a buoy.

For all its glories, Rindge's earthly paradise came under growing pressure soon after he bought it. A wildfire in 1903 destroyed the family's Victorian mansion above Malibu Canyon. The vast ranch was always vulnerable to trespassing, which only increased as more homesteaders settled in the mountains and Southern California's urban population boomed. At low tide, the coast offered firm sands for travel and early maps even show wagon trails edging the ocean. Rindge built his own coastal road from Santa Monica to Malibu Canyon but kept it closed to the public. Nor were individual travelers the only ones interested in traversing the ranch: the Southern Pacific Railroad coveted the natural route along

Coreopsis Coast: Giant coreopsis only grow along a narrow coastal band from San Luis Obispo County south into Malibu, and on the Channel Islands.

the coast for a line between Santa Monica and Ventura.

To foil those ambitions, Rindge began making plans for his own east-west railroad through the Malibu. According to state law, if a railroad already existed then no land could be condemned for the construction of a parallel line. But in 1905 at age forty-seven, Frederick Rindge died suddenly and his wife May K. Rindge took over the ranch. She went ahead with construction of the railroad starting in 1905 and eventually built fifteen miles of the route, which was used to carry barley and other ranch crops to the Rindges' wharf.

Some accounts suggest that Frederick Rindge's dying wish was for his wife to defend his beloved rancho against outside encroachment. If so, it certainly helps explain May Rindge's stalwart, decades-long dedication to that very cause. In the process, she became one of the most important and divisive figures in the history of the Santa Monica Mountains.

During her epic fight against the railroad and later the state highway across family land, Rindge only added to the ranch's legend. There were armed confrontations between her guards and settlers, cattle

rustling incidents and endless court cases, including wins before both the California and U.S. Supreme Courts.

The court cases continued until 1927 when the California State Supreme Court denied a final appeal by Rindge. The Roosevelt Highway finally opened on June 29, 1929. The *Los Angeles Times* promoted the event with an article featuring illustrations of the road's scenery. One large drawing showed a Spanish friar with arms outstretched and a most un-Chumashlike figure wearing a Plains Indian-style feathered headdress standing atop a bluff beholding the Malibu coast

The ceremonies celebrated the completion of this link in the coastal road that would run border-to-border. Perched on the hoods of autos, Miss Canada and Miss Mexico (actually from Oxnard and Santa Monica respectively) watched as Governor Clement C. Young hailed the road's significance, before lighting a small explosive charge that tore apart a barrier across the road. Among the thousands of Southern Californians who traveled the road that day was a young Lawrence Clark Powell, who went on to a legendary career as a writer, publisher and university librarian at UCLA. He took to

Chumash Dwelling: Made of bent reeds and willow, a reconstructed ap stands beneath Boney Ridge at the National Park Service's Rancho Sierra Vista/Satwiwa.

the highway in a Hupmobile roadster and later wrote, "I can still recall the sense of discovery I had during that first day on the Malibu, three hundred eighty-six years after Cabrillo."

But the Malibu would never be the same again. What went unmentioned in the celebratory news accounts was that two people died on the highway within the first sixteen hours of its operation. And a separate article that day lauded the role the new highway would play in the success of a new coastal development, Rancho Malibu La Costa. There were no quotes from Mrs. Rindge.

Derided as imperious and dubbed "Queen May of the Malibu," Rindge can now be seen from a variety of sometimes opposing perspectives. The story of the mountains in the modern era has been one based largely on the battle between private property rights and both public access and environmental protection. In this regard, Rindge clearly can be cast as a hero of anti-government property owners who fought against the establishment of the national recreation area. But Rindge's defense of the Malibu against roadbuilding and urban encroachment helped preserve the Santa Monicas in a comparatively natural state. Her toughness and willingness to struggle for her land also anticipated the role that such women as longtime mountain activists as Susan Nelson, Jill Swift and Margot Feuer would play in the years leading to the park's creation. With mounting legal and financial problems (and the potential for huge profits), the Rindge family eventually did sell off vast tracts of their domain. But thanks largely to May Rindge, *Rancho Topanga Malibu Sequit* was the last of the Spanish land grant ranchos to remain intact.

Adamson House: The Rindge family's Malibu Canyon ranch house succumbed to a 1903 fire but the 1929 Adamson House is a reminder of the family's ownership of the *Rancho Malibu Topanga Sequit*.

A 1920s-vintage Spanish Colonial Revival house set among palm trees commands a rise along the eastern edge of Malibu Lagoon. Longboarders ride the break at world-renowned Surfrider Beach, and across the lagoon the celebrity houses of the Malibu Colony, the first area that May Rindge opened to residential development, extend up the coast. The ranch's old pier, now used for fishing, reaches out into a protected bay known as Keller's Shelter and, to the north, the Santa Monicas rise high above the coast and the gorge of Malibu Canyon.

Known as the Adamson House, it was designed by noted Southern California architect Stiles O. Clements and built as a combination country- and beach-house for the Rindges' daughter Rhoda Agatha and her husband, Merritt Huntley Adamson, who established the family's Adohr Stock Farms dairy. By the

standards of modern-day Malibu mansions and compounds, places more scaled to suit a Medici than a Tapia, the Adamson House is comparatively modest: more farmhouse than palace.

But the Adamson House is also a repository for tilework from Malibu Potteries, the company started by May Rindge that created some of the finest tile made during the twentieth-century revival of this ancient craft in Southern California. The ranch offered a ready resource because the tile was quite literally of the Santa Monicas. High-quality clays from the mountains provided the raw material for the tile and Rindge spoke of using these materials before they were forever lost to development in the hills. Adamson House is lavishly ornamented with pieces from the company that operated for just six years until a 1931 fire seriously damaged the forty-four-thousand-square-foot beachfront factory, which led to its permanent closure the following year.

Given the ranch's huge size, the fact that the Rindge family chose the mouth of Malibu Canyon as the location for its homes speaks to the enduring appeal of this part of the Santa Monicas, a desirability that transcends cultures. The area around the lagoon was the site of Humaliwo (sometimes spelled as Humaliwu), the largest Native American village in the mountains and the place that gave today's Malibu its name.

Humaliwo was the political and economic center both for Chumash in the mountains and the western Tongva, whose territory bordered Malibu Canyon. The largest Chumash villages tended to be situated at spots where streams reached the coast, and the population of Humaliwo is estimated to have been as large as three hundred fifty, more than twenty-five percent of the range's overall population.

Based on midden deposits, it's estimated that the site had been a settlement for three thousand years by the time of the Spanish entrada. Considering the abundance of fish in the lagoons and the easy access both to the ocean for fishing and inland areas for the hunting of game and gathering of acorns and other staples, Humaliwo offered an ideal spot for a community. In many respects, Humaliwo was a regional center. It could be easily reached both by tomol from other coastal villages and on foot along the slopes of Malibu Canyon by residents of inland communities.

The native settlements in the Santa Monicas were hardly isolated. Obsidian from the Sierra Nevada has been found in the mountains and there are accounts of Tongva indicating to Cabrillo in 1542 that they had heard stories of bearded white men arriving in what is now New Mexico, an apparent reference to the Coronado expedition that explored the Southwest from 1540 to 1542. There is also speculation that Chumash from more distant communities used Humaliwo as a resting point before heading out to Santa Catalina Island to trade for steatite, an easily carved stone that was used for pots and bowls.

Such ocean-based trade would have been impossible without the tomol, the greatest technological achievement of the Chumash and the Tongva. Construction of tomols was a demanding job that could take six months and the effort and investment created a hierarchy within the community. Tomol-makers formed an elite guild, with the owner of the boat, often a chief, the most powerful member. For all the romanticization of the Chumash and other California Indians, it was hardly an egalitarian society, with both kinship and wealth as critical determinants of status.

Humaliwo's dome-shaped grass structures sat along the delta of Malibu Creek, the largest watershed in the Santa Monica Mountains. Five times larger than the watershed for Topanga Creek, by name Malibu Creek only runs for less than ten miles below its official starting point below Malibou Lake, but with its main branch, Las Virgenes Creek, it drains a watershed of one hundred nine square miles.

Las Virgenes Creek begins its run about fourteen miles due north of Malibu Lagoon in the Simi Hills, a small range adjacent to and just north of the Santa Monicas. The branches of the creek run between rolling grassland hills, their courses lined by a forest of willow and sycamore. In wet autumns, the forest's golds and oranges stand out sharply against the rounded hills turned green with early rains. The landscape's transition from summer gold to this fresh, green is both a certain sign of the change of seasons and also an indication of the presence of extensive non-native grasses. The now-rare indigenous perennial bunchgrasses of the Santa Monicas actually hold onto their green in most years, even through the long summer dry season that characterizes Mediterranean climates.

Much of the upper creek runs through the former Ahmanson Ranch, site of one of the most contentious and significant environmental battles in California history. For more than forty years this 5,200-acre parcel in eastern Ventura County was eyed for residential development, and in 1992 the Ventura County Board of Supervisors approved a plan for 3,050 residences, golf courses, and retail and commercial space on a portion of the property.

With its proposals to contain urban runoff, monitor the ranch's population of the endangered California red-legged frog and preserve several thousand acres of open space, the plan was touted as an environmentally sensitive new generation of development for

Oak Savanna: Now protected as part of the Upper Las Virgenes Open Space Preserve, these golden hills and oak trees create a classic Southern California tableau.

Southern California. Critics, however, saw it as the last of an era, a gussied-up rationalization of the sprawl and development that for decades had chewed up the mountains and pushed housing farther and farther out onto the once-distant fringes of the Los Angeles area. Ahmanson ran up against the perspective that the time for such development was over because even if the built-from-scratch community proved to be some kind of suburban ecotopia, it would still be appended to a dysfunctional metropolis that would inevitably end up bearing its impacts. Of particular concern was the prospect of urban and golf course runoff into Las Virgenes Creek that would add fertilizers and nutrients that would worsen the Malibu Creek watershed's serious algae and pollution problems. And that foul mix would eventually empty out at Surfrider Beach, where surfers were already suffering a variety of health problems from stream runoff.

Nor was Ahmanson Ranch just another open space area. There were plans for housing on Lasky Mesa that would require the removal of coast live and valley oaks. The mesa was named for filmmaker Jesse Lasky who started shooting movies, particularly epic scenes at this vast expanse, in 1914. Eventually classics such as *The Charge of the Light Brigade* and even *Gone With the Wind* had scenes filmed on the property.

The battle over Ahmanson Ranch became a legal and environmental odyssey, with a succession of lawsuits, the rediscovery of the tiny San Fernando Valley spineflower (a species thought extinct since 1929), the involvement of national political figures on both sides of the issue and an ever-growing grassroots movement, most notably the group Save Open Space. The coalition against Ahmanson combined both NIMBYism and more genuine ecological concerns and was symbolic both of the geographic shift of Santa Monica Mountains

Habitat Edge: Prickly pear thicket bumps up against an oak forest. Prickly pear thrives in parts of the Santa Monicas, and even dominates a small plant community known as cactus scrub.

activism from its West L.A. roots to areas further west in the mountains and also the localization or suburbanization of broader environmental issues. If the rainforest seemed too distant and global warming too complex, here was an easy portal to environmental enlightenment. People were able to look out on thousands of undeveloped acres and envision what another three thousand houses would look like or what an additional forty-five thousand daily vehicle trips on the Calabasas Grade stretch of the 101 freeway would mean to their lives. Once those concerns were raised, it was much easier to introduce the questions of biodiversity or even the watershed problems that were integral to the Ahmanson location.

With opposition growing, speculation about alleged rocket propellant contamination (apparently from the nearby Rocketdyne aerospace facility), and

bond money available for a purchase, property owner Washington Mutual finally opted to sell the land to the Santa Monica Mountains Conservancy in 2003. Now called the Upper Las Virgenes Canyon Open Space Preserve, it is part of nearly fifteen thousand acres of wildlands that form a land bridge to help connect the Santa Monicas to other Southern California ranges. These wildlife corridors enhance the chances for such predators as mountain lions and bobcats to survive.

Las Virgenes Creek has hardly escaped development impacts. South of the 101 freeway, residential areas that had been coveted for the national park fill the valley adjacent to Malibu Creek State Park. Invasive pampas grass with its feathery, seed-bearing plumes spills over onto a few slopes from the neighborhood, but deeper into the protected parkland, there's a sense that the natural order is reasserting itself. Similar to the

Malibu Creek Valley: Broken light filters through intermittent rain clouds as a storm arrives in the heart of the mountains.

Ahmanson property, the feeling here is more meadow-like than mountainous as the creek flows through one of the range's most prominent valleys. Grizzly bears and antelope once ranged through this valley, which was also the site of Talepop, a small Chumash village of forty people that may have only been occupied seasonally.

Most of the time the creeks trickle through the valley, fed in part by neighborhood runoff, but beneath the tangled forest's canopy there's evidence of just how high Las Virgenes and the parallel Liberty Canyon Creek flow following a good rain. Streamside grasses several feet above the channel have been flattened by the current and an assortment of debris—twigs, leaves, plastic bags and tennis balls—collect in dense, dam-like snags against fallen limbs that lay across the creek.

Green and gold-striped *calabazas*, the small pumpkin-like gourd that gave the Calabasas area its name, grow in ground-hugging vines along trails. Up on the slopes, there's a patchwork of vegetation: the frosty-green of purple sage and California sagebrush, the dead brown stalks of the previous spring's mustard and forests of coast live oaks. But inevitably it's the valley oaks that command the scene.

The largest of North American oaks, the trees once grew along bottomlands up and down much of California. The growth of agriculture, particularly in the Central Valley, and residential development decimated valley oak habitat and drained the water table upon which the trees depended. The valley oaks in Malibu Creek State Park grow at the far southern end of the species' range and are easily the grandest of Santa Monica Mountains trees. Limbs twist and curl from stout trunks and climb a good seventy feet into the sky to form wide-spreading canopies that on some trees reach all the way back to the ground. A few valley oaks are almost perfect and symmetrical but others are broken off and stunted, more horizontal than vertical. Hundreds of years old, many bear deep burn gashes from wildfires and are pockmarked by holes created by acorn woodpeckers. These red-capped birds, flashing white patches on their wings as they fly, live in colonies and are commonly seen within the oak canopy. They typically announce their presence with sharp shrieks or staccato tapping as they bore holes into the trees' bark to store thousands of acorns for later feeding.

One local woodpecker gained a measure of pop culture immortality. The cartoon character Woody Woodpecker apparently had his origins at Lake Sherwood, a reservoir in the western part of the range on Triunfo Creek. This bird's persistent tapping on the roof of a house where Walter Lantz was staying proved sufficiently annoying that it inspired the animator to create one of the most enduring, if insufferable, cartoon characters, give or take a mouse or two.

Triunfo Creek, Malibu Creek's other main tributary, begins as seasonal creeks run down the north face of the range's highest ridge, Boney Ridge. Flows continue the length of Hidden Valley, a posh enclave of long white fences and horse ranches. Many are owned by celebrities living the kind of rural life on the urban edge, at one time available much farther east in the range to such stars as Will Rogers, who had a three-hundred-fifty-acre ranch in Pacific Palisades.

At Saddlerock Ranch in Triunfo Canyon, a major pictograph site sits at the base of a landmark formation known as Mitten Rock that is believed to have been occupied by the Chumash as early as 5000 B.C. The rock art here is much more recent however, and features more than one hundred paintings that date back to 500 A.D. One of the most notable paintings shows four men on horseback from what is assumed to be the Portolá party and is considered the only known Chumash portrayal of European explorers. The painting is atypical of the twenty-six known Chumash pictograph sites scat-

Red-tailed Repast: More typically seen riding thermals and soaring high above the mountains, a pair of red-tailed hawks in a clearing squabble over a kill.

Surf Fisherman: While most Southern California beaches offer an almost urban experience, the coastline of the western Santa Monicas remains wild and uncrowded.

tered throughout the Santa Monicas, which display the abstract stylings more typical of the culture's art. The *Handbook of North American Indians* describes Chumash art as "the most interesting and spectacular in the United States." Even within the Chumash world, the rock art of the Santa Monicas is distinctive, thanks to what the handbook describes as its "fantastic anthropomorphic and zoomorphic creatures."

Despite its once remote location, Triunfo Creek forms a corridor long at the heart of the Santa Monicas' cinematic history. Follow the creek, and there's often an inversion of the mountains' real-life history with the movie-making that took place here. Consider Lake Sherwood. Created by a concrete arched dam built in 1904, this Hidden Valley reservoir was rechristened after scenes for Douglas Fairbanks's 1922 *Robin Hood* were filmed among its oaks and sycamores. Legend has it that

the area also was a hideout for the Santa Monicas' real-life *Californio* Robin Hood, Tiburcio Vasquez. Numerous scenes from the *Tarzan* series starring Johnny Weismuller were also shot at the lake. The King of the Jungle has deep ties in the mountains: the 1918 silent version of the story was shot in Griffith Park and *Tarzan* creator Edgar Rice Burroughs bought a ranch in the foothills above the San Fernando Valley that eventually became the community of Tarzana.

Farther downstream, in 1927 Paramount opened a movie ranch along Medea Creek—a tributary of Triunfo Creek—that filmmakers used not only for Westerns but for an unlikely array of global locales: North Africa in *Beau Geste*, Northern California in *Wells Fargo* (a gigantic city set of San Francisco was built), and thirteenth-century China in *The Adventures of Marco Polo*. And Medea Creek was temporarily dammed

Luminous Path: Fallen sycamore leaves begin to cover a mountain trail as autumn comes to the Santa Monicas.

to play the Mississippi River, in a 1931 version of *Huckleberry Finn*.

That dam was only temporary but Triunfo Creek is impounded twice within a short distance as it reaches Malibu Creek State Park. Just beyond the park's western border, it forms Malibou Lake, the centerpiece of a rustic 1920s enclave of homes and a film location for the 1931 horror classic *Frankenstein* (the film's cinematographer Arthur Edeson lived here). Past the lake, Triunfo resumes its flow but loses its name as Malibu Creek officially begins. It's not entirely clear why Malibu Creek doesn't officially start a couple miles deeper into the park where Las Virgenes and Triunfo creeks meet at the main confluence of the entire watershed, but so it goes.

Once in the park, Malibu Creek flows through the Goat Buttes, the park's landmark volcanic peaks, but is quickly captured again by a fifty-foot dam built in 1901 by members of the Crags Country Club. Here it forms Century Lake, which is lined on one side by coast redwoods that the country club planted. Below the dam, the creek bends around one of the buttes then passes through a narrows and into the Rock Pool, a sycamore- and reed-lined grotto set within the volcanic walls. It's one of the classic spots in the mountains, and on outcroppings near the pool, country club members constructed an impressive Bavarian-style lodge.

In 1946, Twentieth Century Fox Studios bought the twenty-three-hundred-acre parcel from the Crags Country Club and renamed it Century Ranch. But the site had been used as early as the silent-film era and notably in 1940 for John Ford's Welsh coal mining drama *How Green Was My Valley*. The studio eventually tore down the country club's lodge in 1955 because it appeared in too many background shots. Like other shooting loca-

Early Development: Houses dating to the 1920s surround Malibou Lake, formed by a dam along Triunfo Creek. Clark Gable and Carole Lombard are among stars who owned homes here.

Rugged Stand-in: For more than a decade, the classic television series *M*A*S*H* filmed on location in the Santa Monicas, giving the range its widest, albeit anonymous, exposure.

tions in the Santa Monicas, Century Ranch proved most versatile, serving as the location for everything from the somewhere-in-the-future *Planet of the Apes* to suburban Connecticut in the Cary Grant comedy *Mr. Blandings Builds His Dream House.* Unlike the many temporary sets constructed at the ranch, the dream house was an actual structure. It was saved and served for years as the headquarters of the Angeles District of the California Department of Parks and Recreation. The building sits in Malibu Creek State Park, which was created in 1974 after Twentieth Century Fox sold the property to the State of California

For all the famous movies that were shot in this area and elsewhere in the range, it was the television show *M*A*S*H* that gave the Santa Monicas their greatest, though still anonymous, exposure. For eleven seasons, the Korean War-era series' opening featured

helicopters approaching over Brent's Peak and the show's exterior scenes were shot on location at a site near the creek. Since it went off the air in 1983 and its final episode drew an entertainment program record of one hundred six million viewers, *M*A*S*H.* has almost perpetually been on the air somewhere in the global village, giving the Santa Monicas an unprecedented ubiquity that even a century of movie filming could never match.

And, after years as an anonymous backdrop, the range would finally have its say. Unbeknownst to most viewers of that final *M*A*S*H* episode, a plotline had to be written into the script after a major blaze began in the mountains and eventually burned through the outdoor set.

Changing Light: A series of ridgelines is revealed in a view looking west across from Saddle Peak as the Santa Monicas take on a blue hue under early morning light.

*M*A*S*H was one of the more overtly political sit-coms ever broadcast, and its proximity to the onetime ranch of Ronald Reagan is another example of the density of the Santa Monicas' cultural associations.

Like many film stars of his era, Reagan was drawn to the mountains, and from his first acting successes to his election as president in 1980, he lived in a series of posh locales: Beverly Hills, Bel-Air and Pacific Palisades. In his autobiography, he recalled riding horses in Griffith Park but it was at the ranch he purchased (now part of Malibu Creek State Park) that some of the key imagery of Reagan's public persona emerged. The Santa Monicas served as the real-life backdrop for his metamorphosis from Hollywood star to historical figure.

In 1951, Reagan bought the two-hundred-ninety-acre ranch in what was then a distant section of the mountains for sixty-five thousand dollars. He raised thoroughbred horses at the property along Mulholland Highway and once said that the ranch was a place where for four days a week he could be a farmer. Reagan dubbed the ranch Yearling Row, the second of his properties to use this name. The original was a Northridge ranch that combined the names of *The Yearling* and *Kings Row*, the two most celebrated movies made by Reagan's first wife Jane Wyman and the future president.

The ranch, at least in a modest way, was the launching pad for his career in electoral politics. While Reagan's political involvement began as president of the Screen Actors Guild and continued as a corporate spokesman for General Electric, in 1958 he helped form the Las Virgenes Municipal Water District. Three years later he gained a seat on the board of the Topanga-Las Virgenes Resource Conservation District in his first election for public office.

Boney Light: Soft February light washes over steep slopes rising to the volcanic outcrop of Boney Ridge in the western Santa Monicas.

Just five years later, Reagan decided to run for governor of California. A reporter was scheduled to visit the ranch and wanted to interview the candidate on horseback. So Reagan put on his usual riding attire, which included jodhpurs. Lynn Nofziger, who later became Reagan's presidential press secretary, took one look and strongly told him to go change into something more ruggedly western to avoid looking like "an Eastern sissy . . . She wants you to be a cowboy. I want you to be a cowboy because that's what the people here will identify with." After a brief protest, Reagan returned in boots and jeans, the kind of cowboy attire that became central to his presidential image, especially when he was out at Rancho del Cielo, the successor to his Santa Monica Mountains spread. That purchase was financed largely with the money that Reagan made when he sold

Yearling Row to Twentieth Century Fox in 1966 for nearly two million dollars, an impressive profit of twenty-nine hundred percent.

Just as he clearly loved the better-known Santa Barbara ranch, Reagan had a deep affection for Yearling Row. His daughter Patti recalls the fences and horse jumps he built and in her eulogy for Reagan, she also spoke of his affinity for the land:

> When I was a child, he took me out into a field at our ranch after one of the Malibu fires had swept through. I was very small and the field looked huge and lifeless, but he bent down and showed me how tiny new green shoots were peeking up out of the ashes just weeks after the fire had

legislature and now much of Point Mugu is preserved as wilderness.

Santa Monica Mountains National Recreation Area was created in 1978, part of an initiative promoted by Walter J. Hickel, secretary of the interior under Richard Nixon. Hickel sought to establish a series of national recreation areas near urban areas. He said the Santa Monicas and its beaches formed "the greatest untapped natural resource" in the Los Angeles metropolitan area. Horace Albright, the pioneering director of the National Park Service from 1929 to 1933, declared, " . . . had the Santa Monicas been located in any other part of America, they would long ago have been set aside in the national interest. Only in California, which boasts such an abundance of spectacular scenery, has it been possible to ignore them."

The Reagan Administration didn't ignore the Santa Monicas so much as it attacked them. Under NPS director William Penn Mott, Jr., the administration stalled funding for land acquisition, a process that to be fair had actually started as part of budget-cutting efforts during the Carter administration and sought to transfer control of the recreation area from the federal government to the state. In the process, key parcels were lost to development, including several in Malibu Canyon

In many respects it's ironic that Malibu Canyon became a stand-in for so many other places in the world. Granted, with its green meadows and chaparral-covered slopes doubling for forested hillsides, it's a plausible Wales and most people lack a specific image of distant lands, whether 1950s Korea or a planet off somewhere in the future run by apes. But for those who know the Santa Monicas, Malibu Canyon is perhaps the definitive location in the entire range, very nearly the literal center and heart of the mountains.

There are places farther west in the mountains that are more pristine. The valley is crossed by two major roads and the creek carries not just fresh runoff but a witch's brew of fertilizers, engine oil and other urban waste that washes down from the watershed's subdivisions and gated communities. Still, there's an indefinable sense of being at some central place.

From rises in the state park, the late afternoon's fog lightly veils Goat Buttes, whose dome-like profiles and craggy surfaces climb with a majesty not seen in

come through. 'You see,' he said, 'new life always comes out of death. It looks like nothing could ever grow in this field again, but things do.'

Despite his personal connection to the Santa Monicas, Reagan's environmental legacy in the mountains is decidedly mixed. The acquisitions of three essential state parks in the Santa Monicas—Topanga, Malibu Creek and Point Mugu—occurred while he was governor, but instead of being protected for their natural beauty these areas were slated for intense recreational development. A landmark environmental battle ensued over plans for Point Mugu. The state had originally proposed a motorcycle track, a golf course, a shooting range and hotels for the 6,554-acre area at the range's far western tip. Those plans were ultimately defeated by the state

King Gillette Ranch: Wallace Neff designed the estate off Mulholland Highway for safety razor mogul Gillette. It later housed a religious order and served as a college campus before coming under public ownership in 2005.

many sections of the mountains. The creek moves lazily through banks lined with sycamores and in the distance the exposed sandstone rock high up on 2,805-foot Saddle Peak takes on a rich, golden light before the sun disappears beneath Castro Crest. The sense of spirituality is only heightened rather than lessened by the one structure visible from certain spots. The elaborately carved towers of a Hindu temple built in the Chola style of southern India stand out pure and white against the numerous shades of green that come with the mountain spring.

As Santa Monica Mountains National Recreation Area came into being, a Malibu Canyon property was envisioned as the logical site for the park's visitor center. With its sprawling configuration and lack of clear identity, the park desperately needed a focal point and the historic King Gillette estate seemed perfectly suited to the role. While unique for its setting and geography, the onetime Chumash village site's complex and controversial land-use history is not atypical in the Santa Monicas.

Gillette, the inventor of the disposable safety razor, bought the land here in 1926 and hired the cele-

brated architect of Pickfair, Wallace Neff, to build a house. With little direction from Gillette, who was away on a yearlong trip, Neff designed a classic Mediterranean compound on the property. Gillette returned from his trip with plants from all over the world to landscape the estate.

Salka Viertel recalls traveling through the mountains to visit the property in the 1930s when Upton Sinclair gave a picnic at the estate for film director Sergei Eisenstein. The irony was not lost on her. "We drove miles and miles over the winding roads of Topanga Canyon to meet the Soviet artists at the mansion of an American tycoon." This acreage has its own movie history too: Gillette sold it in 1935 to Clarence Brown, who directed several Greta Garbo films penned by Viertel, and the land was used in location shoots for the Brown-directed *National Velvet* in 1944.

The estate entered its modern era in 1987 when Soka University, an institution originally founded in Japan that incorporates Buddhist principles into its educational approach, purchased the rundown property from the Church Universal and Triumphant, a religious sect that called the land Camelot. The university then announced plans to expand from a few hundred to more than three thousand students. Park advocates, who hoped to buy the property from the university, later attempted to acquire the land through eminent domain, which led to a protracted legal battle and settlement. Soka won approval for a scaled-down campus before the Sierra Club and Save Open Space filed a lawsuit that sought to limit Soka's ability to carry out its plans. Soka then built a campus in Orange County, which set the stage for the sale of its five hundred eighty-eight Malibu Canyon acres in 2005 for thirty-five million dollars.

Coming soon after the acquisition of the Ahmanson Ranch property, the purchase of the Gillette estate not only represented a new era of protection for the Malibu Creek watershed but the culmination of a decades-long dream for a National Park Service-quality Santa Monica Mountains national park that often seemed to be slipping away. This was, after all, a national park whose visitor center for years shared an office park location with J.D. Power and Associates. The original park plan estimated that a hundred fifty-five million dollars would be needed for land purchases but within two years that estimate had grown to six hundred sixty-seven million dollars. But despite the escalating costs, by 1988 Congress authorized just one million dollars for land acquisition in the mountains and only sixty-eight million dollars had been spent in the ten years since the park's founding. The ongoing public support for the park was evidenced by the coalition of fifty-two different groups that continued to lobby for and ultimately helped garner additional funding from Congress.

Protected Land: Purple sage blossoms on a hillside at King Gillette Ranch. The ranch's five-hundred eighty-eight acres combines with more than four thousand acres in Malibu Creek State Park to create a haven for wildlife and hikers in the heart of the range.

As Malibu Creek flows on toward the ocean, the open meadows and gentle hills of the Las Virgenes Valley narrow dramatically into a gorge. Malibu Creek actually predates the formation of the Santa Monicas and as the mountains were uplifted, the stream continued to follow its path, cutting this chasm in much the same process that the Colorado River carved out the Grand Canyon. The gorge at Malibu Canyon can't compare to the Grand Canyon's one-mile depth or its labyrinthine complexity. But at nearly two thousand feet deep, it is at least comparable to the Grand Canyon's Inner Gorge where the Colorado flows.

The cut reveals a cross-section of the mountains' geology. The canyon's cliffs, with their striations of sandstone, create a tight gap that encloses the creek's tangled riparian forest, as well as Malibu Canyon Road on the western wall. For anyone who thinks of the Santa Monicas as a gentle rolling range, the gorge's ruggedness and scale redefine the mountains.

With its opening to hotter inland areas, Malibu Canyon allows cooler marine air to flow in from the Pacific. Fog pours in and crests over high ridgelines in slow-motion cascades of billowing whiteness. Even on clearer days, the ocean's mist can give the canyon a kind of Maxfield Parrish-style majesty, and the diffused light made the canyon a favorite subject of early California plein air painters. Artists, including leading California impressionist William Wendt, also sought to capture the exquisite composition of the canyon's narrows, where still pools reflect boulders that have tumbled down from the gorge's walls. " . . . At the cliff base," wrote Charles Francis Saunders, author of the 1923 *The Southern Sierras of California*, "is a chaos of rocks curiously ornamented with delicate traceries exquisite as Oriental scripts, the weathered edges of fossil shells embedded there."

At one time Malibu Creek was also celebrated for its southern steelhead trout run. Malibu Creek, along with other coastal streams such as Solstice Creek, offered prime habitat for this relative of the salmon, which like its cousin spends a portion of its life in the ocean before returning to its native stream to spawn and lay eggs in cool pools with gravel bottoms. Unlike

Autumn Creek: Deep in canyons and hidden away in clefts in mountain walls, many of the most beautiful spots in the Santa Monicas remain unspoiled and undiscovered.

Controversial Dam: Historic preservation and the restoration of the steelhead run on Malibu Creek come into conflict at the Rindge Dam, a few miles inland from Pacific Coast Highway.

salmon, steelhead typically survive after spawning. The fish were so abundant that there are tales of locals using pitchforks to catch steelhead. But as a result of declining water quality, river barriers such as dams, and disruptions to the fish's natural cycle, the southern steelhead has been listed as a federally endangered species since 1997.

A key factor on Malibu Creek is the Rindge Dam, the gorge's only major structure. With a steel skeleton constructed of the rails from the Rindge's narrow gauge railroad, the dam was built by the family in 1924 to help irrigate the rancho's farmlands. Thanks to high erosion rates of the watershed's sandstone rock, the reservoir behind the hundred-foot-tall dam filled up with sediment by the 1950s and was decertified in 1967. Steelhead advocates argue that the dam has long outlived its usefulness but continues to obstruct the fish's passage to traditional habitat and spawning grounds farther upstream. They advocate tearing it down. But Ronald Rindge, the grandson of May and Frederick Rindge, counters that the dam has historic value and that the higher water temperatures and low flows in the

Remote Road: Unlike the freeways and commuter shortcuts farther east in the range, routes in the western range are quiet backroad byways, such as Little Sycamore Canyon Road.

upper watershed mean that those areas were never part of the fish's local range. He also says it's pointless to talk about restoring the steelhead above the dam until conditions are improved below the dam; Rindge argues that the fish continued to thrive long after the dam's construction until urbanization in the watershed destroyed water quality.

The creek flows out of the gorge and into a broader coastal plain before reaching the ocean. Surfrider Beach sits along the lagoon and between the Adamson House and the Malibu Colony. Even as efforts to restore the lagoon's ecology and improve nearshore water quality continue, the descendents of the legendary rebel surfer Miki Dora and the pop goddess Gidget ignore health warnings and head out to this classic right break. Considering that surfers routinely disregard shark sightings, microscopic bacteria are unlikely to deter them, especially when the waves are going off.

These aren't the mammoth-sized waves of Oahu's North Shore or Isla Todos Santos off Baja California. But what they lack in size, they make up in

Summer Rainbow: A seastack at Malibu's El Matador State Beach glows red following an unusual summer rainfall that has produced a rainbow over the Pacific.

shape. When south swells reach shore, they begin to lift and form as they hit an arc of submerged cobbles washed down from Malibu Creek. The resulting waves hold their shape for a remarkably long time and rides at Surfrider can last for a minute. Lance Carson, one of the founders of the Surfrider Foundation, the international surfer environmental organization that traces its activism to the pollution issues here at the mouth of Malibu Creek, likened the waves to such natural wonders as the Grand Canyon. Surfrider "breaks like a long string of falling dominoes," Carson explains, adding that waves of this quality "can be found nowhere else in North America."

As PCH continues west past Point Dume, the posh development along the coast gradually thins. The coast takes on an endless-summer quality and, especially late in the afternoon when the sun is setting straight ahead, the windshield glare gives the scene a washed-out, overexposed quality reminiscent of 1960s cinema. Everything is reduced to luminous silhouettes against the bright light: surfers changing alongside the highway, old wooden telephone poles, and gulls and pelicans flying along the shore.

Lawrence Clark Powell, the writer, publisher and celebrated university librarian at UCLA, moved to Encinal Canyon along this coast, and wrote:

> The coast beyond Point Dume is beautiful for its sandy beaches, kelp beds, crumbling palisades and curving line of the Santa Monicas; so immediately beautiful that our television has been dark since we moved. All the hours are lovely in their lights and colors, wind and calm; and if one isn't gardening or gleaning wood on the beach, swimming or walking, he is content to sit and watch the passage of time over the earth.

Powell wrote of the evanescent blues and greens of the ocean and the series of coves and canyons along the coast. He expressed dismay about the encroachment of the city onto this place that he clearly regarded as a paradise, describing the area past Point Dume as "another world, a better world." He wrote of "urbanization spreading like a rash" and the glowing lights of the city as "that monster which feeds on countryside, and which will eat us all in the end. But not quite yet."

The city has continued its advance along the mountain coast, at a pace and in ways that Powell could scarcely have envisioned. But even now there's a point in the drive up PCH where one feels a sense of having reached an escape velocity, of having finally outrun fifteen million people and returned to places that not only Powell would still recognize but perhaps so too would the Rindges, and, maybe, even the Chumash.

Just before the Santa Monicas plunge down to meet the Oxnard Plain at Point Mugu, an old Chumash trail leads up a steep slope above the wetlands of Mugu Lagoon. Now part of Point Mugu Naval Weapons Station, the wetlands were the site of Muwu, one of the largest Chumash settlements along the Malibu Coast. Unlike modern trails, this route has no switchbacks and heads directly up the slope, which is covered with an array of coastal scrub vegetation. The pitch of the ascent naturally slows hikers, thus offering ample opportunity to appreciate the array of plants, which appear at eye level as one looks up the steep trail. Prickly pear cactus bloom with yellow blossoms and chaparral yuccas send up towering stalks with clusters of creamy flowers ten feet into the sky. The lagoon's serpentine channels wind along the shoreline and the ocean spreads toward the horizon with the Channel Islands lined up in the distance.

After climbing nearly nine hundred feet in a half-mile, the trail passes over a rise and drops into a large, open valley of sloping grasslands crossed by creeks marked by stands of oaks. This is the La Jolla Valley, one of the only surviving areas of native grasslands in the Santa Monicas. There's a sense of having made a passage into some separate and hidden place. Giant rye with its wheat-like stalks grows near purple sage, and to see such a place still so pure, to practically taste it, is exhilarating. For all that has been lost in the years since Powell moved to the coast, there are still spots that the city hasn't touched. Not quite yet and maybe never.

In 1928, three years after he was named honorary mayor of Beverly Hills, Will Rogers—the first Hollywood star to become a candidate, albeit rather facetiously, for president of the United States—left the growing glamour capital for the wilder, more open terrain of Rustic Canyon where he owned property. Although his Beverly Hills home had a riding ring and eight-stall stable, Rogers needed additional space for his horses and he eventually acquired nearly three hundred fifty acres of prime Santa Monica Mountains land for his ranch. The ranch also offered considerably more privacy for Rogers and his family at a time when the humorist had become the most popular celebrity in the country.

Explaining the move, Rogers's son James said in 1976, "He wanted to get out of town, he wanted to live out in the country . . . This gave you the country, it gave you the feeling of being out. You could just as well be a million miles from nowhere when you came out here—and yet it was convenient."

Rejecting plans for a formal Mediterranean villa by explaining to his wife that he wouldn't be able to spit in its fireplace, Rogers instead expanded his existing cabin into a rambling ranch house. In a 1927 article announcing Rogers's early plans to move to the ranch, the *Los Angeles Times* contrasted the humorist's tastes with the increasingly ostentatious stylings of houses being built in the mountains. While his ranch was "fresh with the tang of unspoiled 'God's Country,'" other properties were overwhelming the natural feeling of the mountains. "The sagebrush of those ancient hills wears a startled expression, as though unable to comprehend its sudden rise from just plain sagebrush to country estates valued at thousands of dollars per acre."

The interior of the thirty-one-room house became a storehouse of Western art, including Navajo blankets and bronzes and watercolors by Rogers's friend Charles Russell. Rogers also built an enormous stable with a large central rotunda between its two wings. Homespun as he was, the Oklahoma native was also passionate about polo, which rivaled roping as his favorite pastime, and so the ranch had its own polo grounds, on

Bay View: A balcony-like perspective in Topanga State Park takes in a swath of Santa Monica Bay as well as runways and jets at Los Angeles International Airport.

Palisades Retreat: Humorist Will Rogers escaped to his ranch in the Santa Monicas where he was able to live the cowboy life on the fringes of Los Angeles.

land graded by a large herd of mules. Rogers never developed any master plan for the ranch, and instead it evolved more naturally, although with great care, as evidenced by the stonework which featured rock quarried from the Santa Monicas.

With the rugged mountains waiting in his backyard, Rogers would go for rides into the canyons and along the ridgelines of the Santa Monicas. When it suited him, he would use a machete to create new routes through the chaparral. Said his wife Mary, "Will kept adding a new fence, a new corral, a new bridle trail . . . he changes this and that; and the digging, clearing, building and pounding never slowed down while he was here. The ranch was the joy of his life."

The ranch allowed Rogers to turn away from his fame, Hollywood and the sprawl of Los Angeles, and escape into a semblance of the wide open spaces that

fired his spirit and his sense of the country's identity. Seven decades after Rogers's death in an Alaska plane crash, the ranch, now a state park, remains the edge of the frontier in the Santa Monicas as the easternmost trailhead for the sixty-five-mile-long Backbone Trail. The Backbone, a renowned cross-mountain route, travels from the city and into some of the purest places in the mountains before it descends to the ocean near Point Mugu.

The city seems to exert an almost gravitational pull in the first mile or two of the trail. Rather than escaping from the urban, as the Backbone begins its climb into Topanga State Park the perspective on the Los Angeles Basin only gets grander and grander. There's just enough remove from the grittier aspects to render them slightly unreal, almost toy-like. Jumbo jets come down without a sound into LAX and the venting stacks at the oil refineries of Torrance flicker like distant bonfires. Los Angeles, so often incomprehensible from the ground, begins to make sense as a series of commercial clusters lined up along the basin floor from Westwood and Century City and on to the emerald city-silhouette of downtown.

The view also reveals the natural setting of Southern California. Waves roll in, first as gentle ridges on the water then as white foamy lines moving toward the sweep of the Santa Monica Bay shoreline that extends south to the dark rise of the Palos Verdes Peninsula. Santa Catalina Island floats like a gigantic ghost ship between the mists and the ocean off the peninsula's tip. To the east, beyond the dark green of the Santa Monicas, the mountains' fellow Transverse Ranges rise to snowcapped heights above eleven thousand feet. Even Mount San Jacinto, the 11,049-foot Peninsular Range peak above Palm Springs and the Coachella Valley, is visible. From Catalina to San Jacinto, the view takes in one hundred twenty miles of Southern California. And ahead is Topanga State Park, the chaparral-cloaked twenty-one-thousand-acre expanse that forms the largest urban wilderness in the United States.

The stand of chaparral that covers the park is one of the most extensive in the Santa Monicas, a tangled mass that is virtually impenetrable by larger animals and humans alike. Smaller animals, however, have extensive systems of tunnels and pathways through the chaparral. There are all sorts of birds—California thrashers and wrentits among them—that hikers in the mountains hear all the time, in lilting song or rustling among the branches, but only rarely see.

While the Santa Monicas have twenty-six plant communities, chaparral covers fifty-five percent of the range and coastal sage scrub another twenty percent. Statewide, chaparral grows on seven percent of the land area and is the California variation of the brush communities found in the world's other Mediterranean climate zones. Many people find the plant communities uninspiring, yet these assemblages of drought-adapted plants certainly manage to inspire lyrical names: the mattoral of Chile, the fynbos of South Africa's Cape Region, the kwongan of Australia, the phrygana of the Balkans and the maquis of France.

The plants in all five of the world's Mediterranean regions share a set of traits, most notably their ability to thrive in generally nutrient-poor soils, their capacity to survive through an extended dry season and their adaptation to periodic wildfires. Despite the seeming uniformity of landscape, the diversity of species is exceeded only by that of tropical rainforests. In each of these regions, at least half of the plants are endemic species, with southwest Australia having the highest percentage. About one thousand plant species live within the Santa Monicas, with chamise (also known as greasewood), nine species of ceanothus (commonly called mountain lilac) and scrub oak being the most dominant within chaparral.

Despite many parallels, there are also considerable variations in the forms these communities take. Chaparral most closely resembles the maquis of the Mediterranean basin, although the maquis has greater height variation and its canopy is more open. Chaparral is particularly notable for the absence of plants beneath the main canopy of taller shrubs (up to fifteen feet tall), the result, not only because of competition for water and sun, but also because some chaparral plants (most notably chamise, the most abundant of the chaparral plants) may put out chemicals that inhibit the growth of other species. In contrast, the growth patterns in South Africa and Australia are more open, akin to the conditions that exist in chaparral in the first few years after a fire.

Watch the mountains over the course of a year and you'll see what a complex and changing mosaic chaparral truly is. The absence of rain during summer means that plants drop older foliage and have fewer or smaller leaves. But unlike deciduous plants, chaparral plants don't drop all of their leaves, thus conserving water and nutrients that would otherwise have to be directed into the production of new foliage each year.

While still green, there is a faint brownish-red mottling that mixes into the vegetation, and hillsides can appear less densely covered, at least for awhile. When the rains do arrive, the landscape noticeably greens up as the plants become more robust. The scrub seems to swell with moisture. Not long after, typically in January, ceanothus differentiates itself from the rest of the chaparral as each plant puts out thousands and thousands of tiny blossoms that dust the canyon slopes along the Backbone Trail and other mountain locations with pale blues and white. Later in spring, it's chamise that jumps out from the green background with its own burst of white flowers.

Coastal sage scrub—one of the most endangered plant communities in the world—is the other dominant plant community in the Santa Monicas. It lacks some of chaparral's intimidating mystique but is just as critical to the mountains' character and diversity. The "coastal" designation might suggest that the scrub community grows in wetter areas, but in reality it begins to dominate under drier conditions and on sunny, south-facing slopes. In the Santa Monicas this plant community does benefit from a marine influence that delivers extra moisture in the form of fog, but the habitat also extends sixty miles or more inland and some of its individual species survive in desert scrub communities.

In addition to sloping terrain, coastal sage scrub thrives in flat areas below two thousand feet that also happen to be ideal for human activity, be it the farming of generations past or the residential development of our era. Faced with more than a century of pressures, an estimated eighty-five to ninety percent of coastal sage scrub has been lost statewide (its range stretches from San Francisco south into Baja California). The Santa Monicas encompass some of the finest and largest remaining stands of the habitat.

A shorter and more open community, coastal sage scrub is filled with plants less woody and treelike than those in chaparral. Sometimes called "soft chaparral," its plants' foliage lack the leathery thickness of leaves of such chaparral plants as toyon and are instead more supple and therefore also more vulnerable to dry conditions. Unlike chaparral, coastal sage scrub plants are drought-deciduous and go into a scruffy, dormant stage during the dry season, with many species looking nearly as miserable as giant coreopsis during summer. About the only color in the scrub until the rains come is the rich rust-orange that the once cream-colored blossoms of buckwheat take on as the dry season lengthens.

Although the average total annual rainfall in the Santa Monicas is modest, that doesn't mean that its winter storms are always benign. Some rains, certainly, are gentle, drifting and falling to the ground almost like snow flurries. But there are storms that slam into the mountains like waves crashing against the bow of a ship, surging inland and across ridgelines, blowing nearly horizontally across the land, as if the ocean had decided to banish the desert from the mountains.

With the rains, coastal sage scrub undergoes a much more rapid and dramatic transformation than does chaparral. Its most prominent plant is California sagebrush, which despite its name is not a true sage in the mint family but instead belongs to the sunflower family. The sagebrush puts out wispy, teal-green leaves that are soft and nearly rubbery to the touch. As the true sages, most notably purple and black sage, also leaf out, the effect after the long dormant season is as if the land itself is some giant flower that is beginning to open up and bloom. The air becomes saturated with a sweet-yet-penetrating fragrance like menthol. The rich scent results from the fact that coastal sage scrub plants have a higher oil content than chaparral. Even so, the scrub community burns less intensely because of its reduced biomass and a smaller accumulation of leaf debris.

In places, coastal sage scrub creates striking patterns on the landscape, as the frostier greens of the California sagebrush and purple sage create a marbling or mottling effect against the darker greens of chaparral. And at times, coastal sage scrub can become richly textured and garden-like. Bright yellow blossoms of bush sunflowers splash across the greens. The new leaves on laurel sumac, a tree-like shrub found in both chaparral and coastal sage scrub, turn blood-red when backlit, and later in spring, the sages bloom with purple, lavender and white blossoms.

After the Hub Junction, where trails that begin on the Valley side of the mountains converge with routes that nearly reach the ocean, the Backbone passes an enormous sandstone outcrop that rises bold and gold from the surrounding scrub. Part of the twenty-five-million-year-old Lower Topanga formation, Eagle Rock—more rock than eagle in appearance—has a face pockmarked by intrusions of small cobblestones and caverns carved by wind and water erosion. The rock cantilevers out from the slope and serves as a perch for views down Santa Ynez Canyon and across the park. A

Rocky Oaks Meadow: Poppies bloom in the National Park Service's Rocky Oaks, where the spring green of grasslands contrasts with the darker green of chaparral-covered hillsides.

few of the caverns are accessible and large enough to sit in, as evidenced by the vandalism committed upon their walls, which, if one is in a more forgiving mood, may rise to the level of contemporary rock art.

What is notable is the repetition of UFO and extraterrestrial imagery. Alongside images of scorpions, lizards and geographically incongruous inclusions of saguaros are football-shaped spacecraft, including one showing a trio of happy aliens looking like they're out joyriding around the Milky Way. These pictures would seem to be the by-product of Topanga Canyon's long-standing reputation as a UFO hotspot, with reported sightings dating back to the 1940s. The most famous series of sightings began in June 1992 and lasted for more than two years and nearly fifty incidents as witnesses told of the proverbial strange glowing lights and hovering objects.

Preston Dennett's *UFOs Over Topanga Canyon* places Topanga in the pantheon of UFO locations and outlines a number of theories for its prominence: that aliens are able to use the area's deep canyons as a kind of duck blind; that high tech and military activity in the mountains may have drawn extraterrestrials; that the area is a magnetic vortex; and that the Santa Monicas were once part of an ancient, Atlantis-like civilization.

Such talk only reinforces Topanga Canyon's reputation as a fringe community on both the physical and metaphysical edge of Los Angeles. But Topanga has

Plein Air Pastoral: Reminiscent of paintings of early California Impressionists who came to the Santa Monicas, a lone oak stands before the rocky precipice of Boney Ridge.

long been a significant counterculture center for Southern California. Its sense of separateness is tangible, sitting as it does in a deep cleft in the mountains. Old boxcars serve as bridges across Topanga Creek, while oaks and sycamores create a heavy canopy that adds to the feeling of isolation. It's only upon climbing to higher ridges that Topanga is revealed to be not some remote mountain hamlet but actually one that endures only a few miles from both the densely populated San Fernando Valley and posh Pacific Palisades.

Less accessible from the city than the canyon neighborhoods that open to the L.A. Basin, the escape in Topanga is more total, turning it into a haven beyond the reach of the urban—especially when mudslides close the serpentine and often clogged Topanga Canyon Boulevard or Pacific Coast Highway. During 2005, the second rainiest year on record, the boulevard was closed

except for one lane for a few hours a day for months. And those ongoing closures came after an earlier shut-down caused by a three-hundred-fifty-ton sandstone boulder that had rolled off a hillside and landed smack in the middle of the road.

Novelist Carolyn See, the canyon's great chronicler, captures its essence in *Golden Days*, describing a sanctuary of ephemeral waterfalls, blooming ceanothus, stands of lupine and skyscraper-sized boulders, arrived at from the valley only after a stomach-challenging series of twists and turns on Topanga Canyon Boulevard. "We might have been in Australia with just a couple aborigines for company, but instead we could hear Van Morrison, the Doors, windchimes, barking dogs." But she also doesn't ignore the underlying menace of canyon life, whether the survivalist paranoia that balances the utopian optimism or the fires and floods that can destroy

Seasonal Pond: Although home to major reservoirs, the Santa Monicas have no large natural lakes. There are scattered small ponds, and winter rains sometimes create pools that only linger a short time.

in an instant; See lost her own home in the 1993 Old Topanga Fire.

Topanga has drawn an array of seekers and artists almost from the time it was first settled. The very name is poetic and as art critic Antony E. Anderson wrote in 1909, "its cadenced syllables suggested possibilities naturalistic and artistic."

Anderson first ventured out to Topanga at the invitation of the renowned plein air painter William Wendt; Wendt had come to Topanga thanks to the poet and playwright William Vaughan Moody, best known for the play *The Great Divide* and one of the first artists to

canyon: mountain lion tracks, coyotes and menacing poisonous snakes "dealing sudden death, it is said, by (their) very breath." With such thoughts in mind, Anderson actually ends up killing a non-venomous kingsnake that he must have mistaken for a coral snake, a species that doesn't actually live in the Santa Monicas. It was the natural world of the mountains that William Wendt sought to capture, and Anderson writes of his visit to the artist's tent house to see paintings of forests and slopes covered by the golden blossoms of tarweed.

During the 1950s, Topanga became a political refuge of sorts as actor Will Geer arrived in the canyon after being blacklisted. Along with his wife Herta and such friends as poet Carl Sandburg as well as some of Geer's fellow blacklist victims, he began to put on readings and productions, which eventually grew into today's Theatricum Botanicum. Among the performers was folk singer Woody Guthrie, a good friend of Geer's, who arrived in Topanga in 1952 just a month after being diagnosed with Huntington's Disease. Guthrie lived in a stone structure at Geer's compound, then bought some land in lower Topanga that he dubbed Pretty Polly Canyon. But Guthrie's Topanga stay was brief and tumultuous thanks to increasing health problems and an adulterous affair with a local woman that resulted in a pregnancy and his third marriage.

Although Topanga is most typically celebrated for its 1960s music scene, it had its share of counterculture notables at least a decade earlier. Two pioneers of the California Assemblage movement, Wallace Berman and George Herms, lived in Topanga in the 1950s. Berman also gained renown for *Semina*, an avant-garde publication that he printed on a hand press, which featured leading Beat Generation artists and writers. Nor were the lines between the different eras in the canyon so precisely demarcated; Berman and Herms became friends with Neil Young after the singer arrived in Topanga. Berman also had a small role in *Easy Rider* and is part of the gallery of faces on the Beatles' *Sgt. Pepper's Lonely Hearts Club Band* cover.

Topanga provided an even more rustic alternative to the Laurel Canyon music scene, a spirit captured in the blues boogie "Going Up the Country," by the canyon-based band Canned Heat. The Topanga Corral

live in the canyon. Upon arriving in the canyon by stagecoach, Anderson saw a tavern sign painted by Wendt's wife, Julia Bracken Wendt, and discovered a loose community of artists, including the landscape painter George Melcher, who had moved to Topanga in 1906. Anderson was struck by the wildness of the

Tower of Blossoms: In late spring, chaparral yuccas send up ten-foot-tall stalks that bloom with dramatic clusters of flowers. The plant was a key food source for the Chumash.

emerged as one of Southern California's most important musical venues, thanks to a ready stable of canyon musicians and their pals. But Topanga's halcyon days had a dose of Altamont dystopia mixed in with its hit of Woodstock Nation. There were drug busts (including one that nabbed not only Young but also Eric Clapton), guns and Charles Manson, who lived for a period in Topanga with his followers.

Topanga's spirit of back-to-the-land Bohemianism endures, although it is increasingly vulnerable to change. Novelist T.C. Boyle's *The Tortilla Curtain* portrayed the social tensions of the 1990s as Topanga evolved more fully into a bedroom community of increasing affluence. And one of the last vestiges of Topanga bohemia, a loose community of artists and surfers living in shacks in the lower canyon, was evicted after the state parks department acquired the land. In an attempt to capture the Lower Topanga culture and rally support, in 2002 the artists here published a small book of poetry and essays titled *Idlers of the Bamboo Grove: Poetry from Lower Topanga Canyon*. Plans call for a restoration of native vegetation and the wetlands near the canyon mouth and a trail that will lead from the Valley to the Pacific.

The Backbone climbs steeply out of Topanga Canyon from a spot on the old route between the canyon and the San Fernando Valley. The road cuts into a section of the mountains notable for its deep valley and the sandstone gorge of Red Rock Canyon, which despite its name has a range of hues that includes whites and purples. In an account of a 1910 trip, Topanga pioneer Vance Hoyt describes a view from the road into what he called "the heartland of the Santa Monicas. The vista that lay before me was like a great basin, rimmed by a skyline of serrated ridges and peaks . . . "

The Backbone follows Hondo Canyon through dense forests of coast live oaks, bay laurel and stands of chaparral on its way to the summit of one of the mountains that Hoyt described, 2,805-foot Saddle Peak. The high perch of Saddle Peak offers the most commanding view in this section of the mountains. For that matter, the peak's long sloping profile and its exposed areas of

sandstone create one of the Santa Monicas' finest and most traditionally mountainous mountain vistas, especially as it comes into view while driving east on the 101 freeway between Agoura Hills and Calabasas. The trail begins to descend through a tunnel cut through the overhanging ceanothus and bush poppies with their saucer-shaped yellow blossoms, passing numerous small drainages and grottos thick with ferns. It's strange to be so deeply inside the chaparral and to discover the world within its tangle of shrubs. Little apple-like fruits hang from manzanita, whose sculptural, almost polished mahogany-colored limbs are beautiful both to the eye and to the touch. Tubular red flowers with their four long sepals dangle from fuchsia-flowered gooseberry branches lined with glossy green leaves that glisten under the sun, while hummingbird sage blooms in scattered spots within the semi-shade of oak trees.

As it descends, the trail opens up to broader views that look across Malibu Canyon to a long lineup of ridges that fade to the west. Cascades of sticky monkey flower grow out of steep rock faces and butterflies with white wings tipped with orange and black flutter across meadows where the violet blossoms of wild hyacinth move with the breeze, riding at the end of slender stems that extend above the surrounding vegetation.

From the peak's summit and its forest of communications towers, the Backbone descends more than two thousand feet before it reaches a creek shaded with oak, sycamore and white alder at Dark Canyon. Saddle Peak is at the head of what is considered the purest watershed in the Santa Monicas.

Cold Creek flows year-round down the north slope of Saddle Peak, running only a few miles before it reaches Malibu Creek. Archaeological sites indicate that the watershed was occupied as early as five thousand years ago, and in the 1880s, the Stunt family, a trio of brothers from England and their cousin, homesteaded here. Much of the watershed is now protected land, contained within the Mountains Restoration Trust's Cold Creek Canyon Preserve and UCLA's Stunt Ranch Santa Monica Mountains Reserve.

Deep and shaded by a canopy of trees, the canyon remains cool and moist and supports populations of big leaf maple, a tree found more commonly in the Sierra Nevada and in the northwest, where it grows

Streamside Flowers: Growing in wet, shaded canyons, stream orchids and Humboldt lilies are among the most dramatic of the Santa Monicas' flowers.

in forests of coast redwoods. Mixed into the vegetation grow some of the Santa Monicas' most dramatic flowers, including the streamside orchid and Humboldt lily. Its speckled orange petals and elongated stamens that dangle from the upside-down blossom give the Humboldt lily an almost tropical beauty. But with its cascades of water and ferns, Cold Creek comes as close as any spot in the Santa Monicas to the feeling of a temperate rainforest. And the creek and valley's name is well-earned. The basin of Cold Creek Valley is the chilliest part of the mountains, where sub-zero temperatures have been recorded.

As moist and verdant as Cold Creek may be, like other areas in the Santa Monicas it is nevertheless vulnerable to fire, the force that periodically reshapes the mountain landscape. The trunks of many of its oaks are singed black; run your fingers along the wood, they

will become stained with ash even more than ten years after the last fire raged.

Fire resets the clock in the Santa Monicas. If a fire has been contained, that patch of five or ten or one hundred acres will appear different in color and texture from adjacent areas for years to come. That is at least until the entire section of the mountains goes up in flames and it's back to midnight for thousands of acres, such as when the 1993 Old Topanga Fire burned Cold Creek and 16,516 acres from the edge of Calabasas to the sea. What began as a thin plume of smoke turned into a billowing, constantly morphing cloud of reds, oranges, grays and black reminiscent of an erupting volcano.

The mountains' east-west orientation is uniquely vulnerable to Southern California's famed Santa Ana winds. In contrast with the range's prevailing pattern of winds off the ocean, Santa Anas originate in

Valley Vista: Commanding view from Saddle Peak along the Backbone Trail looks beyond sandstone outcrops to Warner Center and the San Fernando Valley.

the desert, then get channeled down the range's north-south canyons, sucking moisture from vegetation, warming and increasing in speed as they go. Santa Anas are primarily an autumn event, and correspondingly the average rate of acreage burned is significantly higher in September, October and November. Just as chaparral has its counterparts in other Mediterranean regions, so do Santa Ana winds and their names too are both poetic and menacing: scirocco, mistral and boreal.

Combine Santa Anas, mature chaparral and an ignition source, and a conflagration will soon follow. Chaparral burns with an almost unimaginable intensity. Thanks to the density of vegetation and the heavy oil content, surface temperatures can reach twelve hundred degrees. That means chaparral fires are four times hotter than grassland fires, which only tells part of the story. When measured for the amount of energy released,

chaparral fires are actually eighty times more intense. And while experts describe such fires as the 1988 Yellowstone blaze as once-in-five-hundred-years events, in the Santa Monicas it can be more like once in a decade. Fires have struck some areas of Malibu eight times since 1925 and during that time an estimated three hundred thousand acres have burned in a range that encompasses roughly two hundred twenty-two thousand acres. Seventy thousand acres have gone up in flames since 1990 alone.

"The Santa Monica Mountains are a true design for disaster," concluded a 1995 California Coastal Commission study.

As adapted to fire as the Santa Monicas may be and as notorious as the range is for its conflagrations, the rate of fires once was considerably lower (and even today there are scattered places that have managed to

Fire Lupine: In the spring after a wildfire, lupine overwhelm and surround the charred limbs of plants burned in the blaze.

escape major blazes for one hundred years). The Chumash deliberately burned sections of the mountains to increase production of their food sources; studies indicate that they may have used as many as two hundred plants for food, and fire also increased forage for deer and other animals that the Chumash hunted. But the overall frequency of fire was considerably lower than during modern times because of the lack of ignition sources, which is to say a growing population of human beings engaged in activities from construction to pyromania; a huge percentage of Santa Monica fires result from arson.

Lightning, the most likely natural source, is rare in the Santa Monicas and when it does occur it is typically accompanied by rain, therefore reducing chances for fire. Lightning certainly occurs less frequently than in the San Gabriels and other fire-prone Southern

California ranges and according to National Park Service studies, no lightning-caused fires occurred in the Santa Monicas over a sixty-year period. Nor did lightning-caused fires burn with the kind of intensity of many modern-day fires primarily because lightning conditions and Santa Anas are mutually exclusive. Instead the fires typically burned for weeks, moving slowly across the landscape.

In many respects, the celebrated fires of the Santa Monicas are a hybrid of natural and cultural phenomena. For one thing, the significance of fires, at least in the public imagination, is not a function of acreage or habitat burned. There have been so many massive fires that size alone doesn't equal notoriety. Acreage is not a measure but the number of homes lost is, trumping even lives lost.

The 1961 Bel-Air fire which destroyed nearly

Devastating Beauty: A fire burns through live oak woodlands. The oaks are adapted to periodic wildfire and many will endure several blazes over the course of their lifetimes.

Fire Plume: Smoke hangs ominously over the Santa Monicas. The dried grasslands and mustard in the foreground provide fuel but don't burn with chaparral's intensity.

five hundred homes is part of the city's popular mythology. It is to other Santa Monica Mountains fires what the Academy Awards are to the People's Choice Awards. The fire's perimeter encompassed the heart of celebrity Los Angeles, from Mulholland Drive on the north to Sunset Boulevard on the south and Benedict Canyon on the east to Sullivan Canyon on the west. The *Los Angeles Times* showed Kim Novak hosing down her home's roof, and Zsa Zsa Gabor dug through the rubble of her four-hundred-thousand-dollar home while wearing a forty-carat diamond ring. The paper described the fire's victims who took shelter in both Red Cross facilities and Beverly Hills hotels as "the wealthiest class of evacuees since the Russian revolution."

Although one news account described the Santa Anas that helped fan the November 1993 Old Topanga Fire as having "the capricious will of the mythological

furies," for all their intensity, fires in the Santa Monicas tend to be ritualized in their sequence of events: the Santa Anas begin blowing; a fire starts at an inland spot in the mountains; the flames are blown toward the ocean through canyons and follow nearly identical routes of previous blazes; evacuations take place; and firefighters make a heroic last stand at Pacific Coast Highway. And at the beach, deer, horses and other animals that had fled to the coast ahead of the fire and residents all mingle at the edge of the ocean as the fire rages.

By most accounts the Old Topanga Fire was faster and more furious than almost any fire in the range's history. With relative humidity as low as seven percent, the fire spread from an acre to two hundred acres in ten minutes and burned a thousand acres within the first hour. Smoke rose thirty thousand feet into the sky and embers touched off new fires more than two-

Water Drop: Having already picked up a belly full of water, a Superscooper swoops down to attack a ridge-line hot spot.

and-a-half miles in advance of the fire. When the fire approached, houses trembled as if an earthquake was occurring before bursting into flames like matches, according to one firefighter. The fire eventually destroyed 388 buildings, more than ten percent of the total number of structures determined to be at risk by fire managers when the blaze started. During one twenty-eight-minute stretch in mid-afternoon, the fire consumed twenty-two hundred acres, a rate of seventy-five acres per minute and flames reached PCH within four hours of the first reports of smoke.

Except for post-fire coverage of the mudslide threat when rains come, the mountains themselves receive little attention. The land is blackened and trees are charred. Virtually every bit of greenery is gone, and boulders and rock faces long covered by chaparral are exposed. The very structure of the mountains is revealed

again. A layer of ash covers mountain neighborhoods and sometimes incinerated leaves of manzanita and other plants drift into yards miraculously intact only to pulverize at the slightest touch.

It's difficult to imagine new life springing from so much devastation but the recovery begins almost immediately. Even as the land continues to burn, fire beetles, drawn by heat and smoke that sensors on their thoraxes detect, fly to the blaze from miles away. They come to the scene to feed on plant tissue no longer protected by sap and to mate. The female lays her eggs in burnt wood, which provides a food source for the larvae. Within days after the fire, the chaparral and coastal sage scrub communities begin their recovery. Leaves emerge from the singed trunks of coast live oaks and although everything above the surface has been charred, shrubs such as laurel sumac survive underground and re-sprout

Immediate Aftermath: Wildfire smoke blots out the sun and creates eerie light, turning a burned slope into a hellish vision of destruction.

directly from their root crown burls. One of the most beautiful sights in the mountains is the play of clusters of fresh green leaves growing from the base of a charred stump against the blackened landscape as chaparral plants come back to life. Not only are there benefits for the plant community but for the surviving wildlife too. The productivity of chaparral, in terms of forage, can go down as the stand ages but its new growth is high in protein and considerably more nutritious for deer and other animals.

Despite the intensity and ferocious heat of wildfires, temperatures even a few inches down are considerably cooler, allowing both plants and seeds to survive. The seeds of many plants, including chamise and ceanothus, require fire to germinate: some need exposure to at least two-hundred-fifty-degree temperatures while others respond to chemical cues from smoke and burnt wood. The heat or chemicals rupture the waxy coating of the seeds, so that when rains come the seeds'

contents are exposed to water and the growth process begins. What is also remarkable is that seeds can remain viable for decades until they receive the proper stimuli.

By the following spring, assuming there have been decent rains, the land comes alive in ways unimaginable—either before or after the fire. With the canopy of shrubs no longer there to block the sun, a host of flowers, some that haven't been seen for generations, color the land; following the Old Topanga Fire, a species of phacelia emerged in one mountain area that hadn't burned for at least a century. The display is made more beautiful because the carpet of flowers surround the twisting, blackened stems of chaparral plants in a tableau of death and rebirth akin to a resurrection. Patches of Parry's phacelia, their deep purple petals made even more

Scorched Earth: A clear morning reveals the intensity of heat in a chaparral fire. Every bit of foliage has burned and the flames have even turned rocks black.

Cold Creek Hot Spot: Cold Creek Canyon with its dense vegetation cover burned with an unimaginable intensity, especially as flames moved up the steep canyon slopes.

Miraculous Recovery: New shoots and leaves poke through burned sycamore bark shortly after fire.

vivid by a white speckled center, paint slopes and play off the reds of Indian pink and the orange of California poppies. Less common is the brick-red fire poppy, which appears almost exclusively after fires.

Every so often news accounts report strange wildlife happenings in the Santa Monicas. A black bear is spotted in an Agoura Hills backyard. A mountain lion is seen furtively prowling an Encino neighborhood.

While the public greets these sightings as one-off, evening news curiosities, others find some hope that the Santa Monicas are functioning as a viable ecosystem. Still, at least for mountain lions, it's a tenuous existence. Most of the range's larger predators have been exterminated. Wildlife biologists were thrilled when the lone male lion in the Santa Monicas and a female produced a litter of four cubs in fall 2004 and were sur-

prised when another cougar took residence in Griffith Park earlier that year. But such excitement is invariably tempered by news of road fatalities. Or the discovery a few months after the cubs' birth of two dead mountain lions in nearby Simi Valley after apparently ingesting the corpses of rodents that had been poisoned with anticoagulants. The fragility of the mountain lions' survival in the Santa Monicas was made even more graphic when the male lion later killed the cubs' mother, further reducing his mating options and increasing the chances of inbreeding.

At a hundred fifty pounds, the male lion that rules the Santa Monicas is by far the king of the mountains—assuming he behaves himself. Despite years of study and research of the animal, a permit was taken out in 2003 to have the lion tracked by dogs and shot. The lion had apparently forsaken his more common prey, mule deer, and killed five goats kept in a Malibu Canyon enclosure behind a five-foot-high fence, a quick hop for an animal with a fifteen-foot vertical leap and that can cover forty feet in a single bound. In an 1892 account of a mountain lion hunt, Los Angeles pioneer Arturo Bandini describes a big cat as "rising like a winged creature high above the greasewood and chaparral, ground scent for the dogs is barely left so daintily does he alight; the hounds must use the slightly-tainted air for their guide." After the 2003 incident, hunters shot at the lion but the goats' owner, a controversial land speculator in the mountains, said that he only intended to scare the cat away, not kill it.

As formidable as the lions can be, for much of the range's history it was the grizzly bear that ruled the Santa Monicas. The grizzly is one of North America's most iconic animals, a massive predator that stands eight feet tall on its hind legs and can weigh up to nine hundred pounds. Although the bear remains on the California flag, the state's last grizzly was killed in 1922, turning the flag into a rather sad and morbid symbol of the environmental destruction that has taken place.

The Santa Monicas provided ideal habitat for the giant bears thanks to abundant steelhead in its creeks and ample forage; for all their notoriety as predator, grizzlies are also opportunistic and omnivorous feeders. Grizzlies thrived in chaparral and grassland environments and were so common in the mountains that they became a serious problem for ranching operations in and around the Santa Monicas.

Not surprisingly, grizzly bears were regarded as a problem to be eliminated. Mountain men hunted down the bears in the Santa Monicas and a popular sport and gambling enterprise was to throw bulls and grizzlies into a ring and let them fight to the death. Symbolic of the changes coming to Southern California, the last of these battles in Los Angeles took place in 1860, the same year that the first baseball game was played in the city.

Southern California Winter: Significant snows are rare in the Santa Monicas but the range does offer outstanding winter panoramas, such as this Boney Ridge view across the Oxnard Plain to the Topa Topa Mountains near Ojai.

Castro Crest: Nowhere is the Backbone Trail more backbone-like than along Castro Crest, where sandstone fins create one of the Santa Monicas' most distinctive landmarks.

California mythologizer Major Horace Bell wrote several accounts of grizzly bear incidents. In one near Encino, he describes an encounter between the prominent Santa Barbara *Californio* Don Jose Ramon Carillo and a bear. A capable swordsman, Carillo relied on his saber and dueled the grizzly, parrying and thrusting with what, if legend is correct, must have been a very angry and confused bear. Bell also wrote about the most famous grizzly incident in the Santa Monicas, which took place in 1853 when mountain man Andrew W. Sublette encountered a pair of bears in Malibu Canyon.

The Kentucky-born Sublette was from a family of prominent western explorers and fur traders. He came to California in 1849, where he tried mining with little success, then started grizzly-bear hunting among other pursuits. Grizzlies were found throughout the range and Sublette shot a bear in Cahuenga Pass near the site of the Hollywood Bowl. But in the Malibu Canyon incident, Sublette and his hunting dog Old Buck killed one grizzly but then were attacked by a second before he could reload his rifle. Sublette's hunting partner was nearby and described a vicious struggle as the mountain man wielded a knife against the grizzly and its curving four-inch claws while Old Buck bit at the bear. Sublette stabbed the bear to death but was seriously wounded and died after being brought to Los Angeles. Legend has it that Old Buck, who had helped save Sublette from another grizzly attack earlier in 1853, died a few days after the funeral without ever leaving the grave.

The absence of the larger animals doesn't mean that mountain wildlife lacks diversity.

More typically found in deserts, ringtail cats, actually a distant relative of pandas, are almost never seen, but bobcats, a true feline, have adapted well to the

Wild West: Near the end of the Backbone Trail above Sycamore Canyon, the western end of the Santa Monicas are undeveloped, with only non-native mustard as evidence of a human presence.

increasing human activity in the range. Hike in the Santa Monicas and there's constant activity on the ground and in the air. Western fence lizards are a frequent sight along trails, scurrying ahead of the hikers' footfalls, while alligator lizards, up to two feet long from the nose of their triangular-shaped heads to the tip of their tails, are less common. The range's one year-round hummingbird, the Anna's hummingbird, whirs through the air, its wings sending out a staccato buzz. With their glistening red throats and flecks of green, they are perhaps the most gorgeous of the mountains' birds. But they are also tough and territorial, chasing away rivals with unimaginable bursts of speed and agility and ferocity, reminders of the kind of survival dramas still taking place in the Santa Monicas, just sometimes on a smaller scale.

The tarantula hawk is every bit as fearsome as

it sounds: a copper-winged wasp with shiny black legs and a pair of curling antenna coming out of a head outfitted with a pair of jaws designed to help wreak havoc on its namesake prey. The tarantula hawk employs a rather Gothic predatory strategy. The female wasp searches out tarantulas or draws them from their dens by vibrating the web at the entry. When the tarantula emerges, the wasp tries to paralyze it with a sting. Then things get creepy, kind of a cross between the myth of Sisyphus and *The Silence of the Lambs*. The hawk, displaying remarkable strength and perseverance, drags the paralyzed and much larger tarantula to a hole, sometimes making its way uphill and through deep sand. The wasp then lays eggs on the spider's abdomen. Soon after, the larvae hatch and begin feeding off the still-living tarantula until metamorphosing into adulthood.

The Santa Monicas' nine native amphibian

California Newt: California newts spend most of the year out of water, and shelter in moist areas beneath logs and rocks. When rains come, they can be seen migrating to pools.

species (including the federally endangered California red-legged frog) are also a curious lot. For one, the California treefrog, which ranges from San Luis Obispo County into Baja California, has made an intriguing adaptation. While many cold-blooded animals bask in the sun, such behavior tends to be common in animals clad with protective scales, such as turtles, lizards and snakes. But the California treefrog, protected just by its membrane-like skin, can be found resting in full sunlight for as much as eight hours a day, even in summer.

Within the clear but tannin-colored waters of some of the range's streams, California newts work their way through pools that offer ample hiding places among sandstone boulders. For all their sloe-eyed cuteness, these newts harbor a dark secret. Their skin has a neuro-toxin that is similar to the substance found in the puffer fish, and is one of the deadliest poisons known in any animal. Not that they make good eating, but a single five-inch-long newt could kill an adult human.

The newts and other amphibians face a variety of human-created challenges to their survival. With their thin skin membrane, through which they are able to draw oxygen from the water, amphibians are highly vulnerable to changes in water quality; in the Santa Monicas, runoff from residential development delivers fertilizers, pesticides and motor oil into mountain streams. The introduction into watersheds of exotic predators such as crayfish has also been devastating, while mosquito fish, first brought into the area as a biological control for mosquitoes, have upset the mountains' stream ecology by preying heavily on newt larvae. And poaching by collectors is such a serious problem that some officials in the mountains believe that the range's amphibians almost have to be treated in the same manner as rare archaeological sites and ask that precise locations of populations not be revealed.

Despite its name, for most of its sixty-five miles the Backbone Trail doesn't run along ridgelines. From Malibu Canyon, however, it climbs nearly fourteen hundred feet in less than two-and-a-half miles to reach the eastern end of Castro Crest. The crest forms the high divide that dominates Malibu, and it tops out at 2,824-foot Castro Peak, one of the rainiest spots in the range. The crest takes in views of both the ocean and inland sides of the range, looking down long slopes of dense chaparral in Corral Canyon to the south and Malibu Creek State Park's remarkably unspoiled Kaslow Natural Preserve on the north. Tight-roping along the divide, here the trail lives up to its Backbone designation. It even looks rather spine-like, thanks to

slabs of tilting sandstone that rise up out of the chaparral and scrub, as if the very vertebrae of the mountains were poking through. In a few spots, the sandstone has eroded to delicate, cathedral-like turrets but the effect in most areas is something between Stonehenge and Cadillac Ranch.

As it reaches Corral Canyon Road, the Backbone again drops off the high ridge and into a stand of chaparral, even though the fire road continues along the crest to the summit of Castro Peak. An intimidating set of signs on an iron gate that blocks the connection to the Latigo Canyon stretch of the Backbone declares that hikers will be trespassing if they continue past this point. The signs were put up by a local landowner who has threatened to pave this stretch of the trail even though National Park officials contend the gates are illegal.

Disputes centered on property rights had been a common theme even before the national recreation area's creation. The Santa Monicas came under growing pressure as Los Angeles boomed in the 1880s. More homesteaders began to settle in the mountains and by 1908, only thirty thousand acres of public land remained available for claims. The final claim was filed in 1923

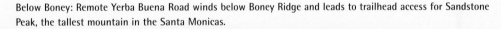

Below Boney: Remote Yerba Buena Road winds below Boney Ridge and leads to trailhead access for Sandstone Peak, the tallest mountain in the Santa Monicas.

Red Shank: Comparatively rare in the Santa Monicas, red shank grows in scattered areas, including Cold Creek Valley and below Sandstone Peak. It's notable for its peeling bark.

and was the last of two hundred thirty thousand acres transferred from federal to private hands. This milestone marked a closing of the frontier in the Santa Monicas and even the pro-development *Los Angeles Times* sounded wistful at the prospect. "This last claim recalls to memory the early days of the State when the Santa Monica Mountains country was the haven for cattle rustlers, road agents, bandits and all the rest of the members of those old pioneer robber bands which gave peculiar flavor to California's early history."

As more settlement came to the mountains, the earliest rumblings for government protection of the range began. The Rindge family was behind some of the first proposals to establish a forest reserve, drawing the ire of both homesteaders and the *Times*. The proposal was decried as an attempt by the family to further lock up the mountains for their own benefit and to restrict future

development—a charge frequently leveled at open space advocates in our time. As the *Times* put it, "Would it not be balm to your soul for Uncle Sam to create at your request a forest reserve extending along the back of this magnificent land-holding, thus adding to your exclusiveness and practically doubling your domain . . . "

The Rindges weren't the only Southern Californians looking to establish protections in the Santa Monicas. In 1914, a hunter named DeMoss Bowers advocated a preserve that anticipated Santa Monica Mountains National Recreation Area by more than sixty years: "Why not establish a game preserve in the Santa Monica Mountains, a natural habitat of wild animals? A great game preserve of say, fifty by fifteen miles in extent, which would be a wonderful attraction, and where we could use the camera instead of the rifle?"

By the 1920s, the Santa Monicas were increasingly seen as a place of development, both a largely untapped resource for the ever-booming metropolis and as a setting for a new kind of utopian city. In *These Waiting Hills*, one of the few books written specifically about the range, John Russell McCarthy both celebrates the beauty of the Santa Monicas and invokes a kind of manifest destiny: "Rome, from the warm cosy spot where the wolf gave suck, climbed out upon her seven hills and challenged the world. Los Angeles now adventures upon her seven hundred hills and invites the world."

McCarthy saw the city as a monster of sorts that could be escaped not only by the rich but increasingly by the middle class too. The mountains would allow people to live close to nature while still having the advantages of the city within reach. McCarthy rhapsodizes about sunsets, roadrunners and wildflowers, and laments the intrusion of automobiles ("gas buggies") into the wilds, once the exclusive domain of equestrians and happy wanderers. (His concerns about the auto were hardly misplaced considering one 1910 article celebrated a weekend explorer hooking a trout in Topanga Creek while still seated in the comfort of the driver's seat.) At one point, while exploring in Topanga Canyon, McCarthy reacts with dismay that after walking for three hours from a point seventeen miles outside the city, he comes upon a Los Angeles city limits sign. Then he envisions the possibilities of what he calls the "dream city":

> Hills, canyons, trees, a stream, no house in sight—this is a glorious part of the city. Los Angeles! One hopes you will keep on using this part of your town for something besides apartment houses and department stores. Why should a town be all streets and tenements and markets? Take in all the hills, canyons and mountains you can reach or buy.

Dana W. Bartlett, a preacher who founded the social service organization the Bethlehem Institute, was a champion of the City Beautiful movement in Los Angeles and the role that the mountains could play in creating what he dubbed "the better city." Bartlett was less boosterish in outlook, acknowledging that "the word real is synonymous with real estate" in Los Angeles.

Befitting his spiritual outlook and his outreach work with the poor, he saw the Santa Monicas (which he never mentions by name) as a place of spiritual uplift for the people of Los Angeles. "It is a great, natural, God-given amenity, for the perpetual pleasure of all the people."

Much of his appreciation came as a result of his own move to a small farm on the flanks of the Santa Monicas. In his 1923 book *The Bush Aflame* (a biblical, not botanical, reference), he wrote,

> From the love of humans in the man-built cities, I have come to love the God-made world just beyond the city wall. Out there we have our home on

Mediterranean Vision: Vineyard leaves in Newton Canyon below Backbone Trail turn orange in late autumn in a scene reminiscent of the Tuscan wine country.

Tilted Rock: Sandstone outcrops along Backbone Trail reveal dramatic as once horizontal strata are tilted to vertical.

the mountain side within sight of the big city, yet far enough removed so that the noise and clatter form a murmur full of music, like the sound of distant waves beating on a rocky shore.

Bartlett was certainly unafraid of progress and wrote approvingly that "the countryside and the city have joined hands." He celebrated the coming of Mulholland Drive for "the panoramas of snow-clad mountains, of valleys and sea and towns" it would open and took pleasure in the exotic plantings and extravagant architecture of his rich neighbors at the canyon's mouth—apparently Beverly Hills. In a 1925 article illustrated with photos of storybook cottages with cobblestone chimneys and red-tiled roof Mediterranean houses, Bartlett wrote of the day when two hundred fifty thousand people would live in "artistic homes" in the Santa Monicas. Influenced by the Craftsman ideal, Bartlett saw the home as a place of personal expression and a sanctuary for both the intellect and spirit, especially in combination with a proximity to the natural world.

"Why not live where singing birds hold songfestival through the mating months of spring, and the chaparral is abloom in waves of color?"

The long, crenellated volcanic rampart of Boney Ridge thrusts high above the western part of the Santa Monicas. Seen from Rancho Satwiwa on the north, the ridge seems to break free from the surrounding slopes. From the west it crowns the Santa Monicas to create the range's most classic mountain vista.

Its vertical rock faces make Boney seem largely inaccessible, but the ridge and the range's highest point, the geologically incorrect Sandstone Peak, can be climbed via the Backbone. There's a short, steep ascent from Yerba Buena Road but the more satisfying approach is via the Mishe Mokwa Trail, which dips into Carlisle Canyon, passing by palisades of exposed reddish rock known as the Echo Cliffs. After crossing a trickling creek, the trail climbs to rejoin the Backbone for the final approach to Sandstone Peak, entering a large hanging valley thick with red shank, an upper

chaparral plant notable for its peeling bark and scarcity in the Santa Monicas.

The lower elevation views of Boney Ridge offer no hint of this valley where rock outcrops poke above the red shank, and wild hyacinth, owl's clover and goldfields carpet gaps between the shrubs. Although the ridge is barely three thousand feet, the final approach to Sandstone Peak, a steep passage up an exposed, jagged turret of rock crusted with frosty green and rust-colored lichen, provides a brief taste of above-the-timberline mountaineering. The panoramic view extends from the Channel Islands on the west and looks east across the Transverse Ranges to the snow-covered crest of Mount San Gorgonio, Southern California's tallest peak at 11,502 feet.

"All the world is spread like a map below," wrote poet Madeleine Ruthven in *Sondelius Came to the Mountains,* a 1934 collection of poems that celebrates the Santa Monicas.

Ruthven was a screenwriter for Paramount and MGM in the 1920s and 1930s and married Reuben Warriner Borough, a journalist who edited Upton Sinclair's *End Poverty in California* (EPIC) newspaper in the 1930s and later ran unsuccessfully for the U.S. Senate in California. Ruthven describes the mountains with a passion and detail that is exceedingly rare among the writers who have lived in and explored the mountains. Hers is the unspoiled range of the western Santa Monicas, from sycamore-filled canyons to the high crags of Boney. The mountains are almost untouched, home only to those that Ruthven believes truly belong here, such as the pioneer homesteaders and Hubert, a rancher who makes "Boney Mountain Juleps," created from a neighbor's moonshine and the local sage. Ruthven describes skies of desert blue and a profusion of wildflowers so extreme that she opens the volume by expressing relief that she didn't first come to the mountains in spring. "Spring is too prodigal in these mountains/To be accepted at first meeting."

What emerges in many passages is Ruthven's joy at her ongoing discovery of the mountains. Though written seventy years after William Brewer's travels and thirty years after J. Smeaton Chase's fabled ride up the coast, the mountains still come across as an Eden-like frontier. She writes of chaparral tugging at her clothing

Sky Over Sandstone: Traffic on the Ventura Freeway creates a necklace of lights beneath the darkened profile of Sandstone Peak as storm clouds break up to create a dramatic winter sunset.

as she hikes through canyons and her newfound ability to distinguish between plants that initially all looked the same to her by noting their varied textures and shades of green. For all her growing awareness and mastery of the Santa Monicas, she doesn't seek to tame the mountains and recognizes her otherness from the range's animals, whom she cannot see but knows are watching her from the brush. Ruthven writes that these creatures don't accept her while the hawks and vultures that circle overhead don't trust her.

Ruthven holds a special reverence for Boney Ridge. She writes of a great fire leaping over the ridge and of visiting a cave with pictographs painted with a mixture of Boney's red rock and deer tallow. But it is in this poem that Ruthven also hints at the changes coming to the mountains. While painted figures are still visible on the wall of the caves, the red hues as vivid as trumpet flower, Ruthven also notes that vandals have chipped away at the rock art and stolen the fragments.

Ruthven's depiction of the Santa Monicas in a pristine state is perhaps rivaled only by the landmark plein air paintings completed here in the 1890s.

The Santa Monicas played a pivotal role in the evolution of California Impressionism, one of the region's most celebrated schools of painting. Ever ready to celebrate his earthly paradise, Malibu rancho owner Frederick Rindge brought artists William Wendt and George Gardner Symons to the ranch to portray scenes of the Malibu. The two painted nearly eighty works while at the ranch in 1897, capturing coastal landmarks, such as Wendt's *Bluffs of Pt. Dume* and various mountain locations including Malibu Canyon and Symons's majestic view of the range's high country in *Old Bony*. When Wendt exhibited some of his Malibu paintings at the Art Institute of Chicago in 1898, his portrayals of the play of light on the golden hills (most of these works were done in summer and fall) was so vivid that one critic wrote it was initially hard to believe the hues were real.

Wendt's and Symons's works at Malibu are considered by many to be the forerunners of the California Impressionist style, the state's first homegrown artistic movement. "Their adoption of the style can almost be dated to 1896-97, when they were painting together on the Malibu Rancho near Los Angeles," wrote Nancy Dustin Wall Moure in her book *California Art: 450 Years of Painting & Other Media*. Despite such auspicious beginnings, comparatively few early paintings of the Santa Monicas exist, mostly because of limited access to the Rindge ranch. When Michael Zakian, director of the Frederick Weisman Museum of Art at Pepperdine University, curated the exhibition "Historic Landscapes of Malibu," he located only fifty works from the period between 1890 and 1940. But among the works were paintings by such leading Southern California artists as Millard Sheets, Elmer Wachtel and the watercolorist Emil Kosa, Jr., a movie art director who likely painted scenes of Malibu Canyon during breaks in location shooting, according to Zakian.

These early paintings of the Santa Monicas provide one of the truest visions and records of the mountains before development. Early black-and-white photos of the Santa Monicas invariably have a ghostly aspect about them. The paintings are of course more subjective and less documentary in nature, especially when artists compress perspective or shift ridgelines to improve composition. Wendt, however, said that he chose not to alter the scenes he painted and instead selected locations for their inherent composition. "I

don't believe in meddling much with nature's intentions. Her ideas are good enough for me."

Altered or not, the early paintings capture the spirit of the mountains, offering a standard of sorts for modern devotees of the range seeking to both understand and find the essence of the Santa Monicas during a time when roads, ridgetop mansions, power lines and communications towers can intrude on that vision. Still, lovers of the mountains, by necessity, have developed a remarkable ability to edit out many of these obstructions. Come back from a hike and it's the sensations that endure: the scent of the chaparral on a foggy morning, the trilling call of a spotted towhee, the spray of pink of prickly phlox against a golden sandstone face and the baying courtship of a pair of bobcats. What lingers in the memory is pure.

There's no denying that humans have been altering the mountains for thousands of years, although the rapidity and scale of change over the past hundred fifty years is of a different magnitude. Despite the many mistakes and compromises that have been made, the Santa Monicas can be still understood and appreciated as a wild place. And it is perhaps imperative that they be approached that way. Numerous locales survive in the mountains in a comparatively unaltered state, both existing largely at a remove from human activity yet also serving as touchstones for those seeking to experience the very soul of the mountains.

For all the cultural achievements that took place in the mountains, the greatest of all cultural achievements may have been the saving of such places and the preservation of the Santa Monicas themselves. The mountains will endure long after we are all gone just as they existed outside of any human consciousness and awareness for millions of years before the arrival of its first peoples. But in our time, sad as it is to say, the Santa Monicas—the living breathing mountains with their processes of life and death and elaborate systems of relationships among plants and animals—would not continue to exist even in a compromised form without the consciousness that has gradually emerged over the past hundred years. With or without us, the range has an intrinsic value all its own. If, as a result, we are able to experience the mountains and retreat into its beauty and reconnect to nature, to be physically challenged by the

La Jolla Valley: Like some hidden kingdom, the native grasslands of La Jolla Valley spread out beneath the high rampart of Boney Ridge.

very geology and intellectually and spiritually enlightened by a greater understanding of our place in the natural order, that too has an immeasurable and more immediate value. But the true achievement is in appreciating that such benefits are not the prime motivation to preserve the Santa Monicas, but spring from a willingness to surrender to higher values than the self.

As the Backbone Trail nears the end of its run in Point Mugu State Park, the path comes down in a series of long, almost ceremonial switchbacks through rounded hills covered in coastal sage scrub and chaparral. It drops nine hundred feet in these last few miles to the Pacific and the air mingles the familiar scent of sage with a whiff of salt air blowing in off the ocean. Towers

of yucca blossoms punctuate the brush with exclamation marks of spring and the trail's switchbacks etch Vs across benches of blooming chamise. Boney Ridge stands tall and ruddy, warmed by the light of late afternoon, while in the distance Anacapa and Santa Cruz islands line up, shadowed and hovering in the channel mists. The crash of the waves is muted and distant as a pod of dolphins passes offshore and a lone raven dances atop the currents rising off the hills. Here the Santa Monicas are beyond the city, no longer measured by jurisdictional boundaries but by their position within the order where they have always existed. A place somewhere between ocean and desert and sky.

Acknowledgments

One day Tom brought over a torn and battered file stuffed with yellowed newspaper clippings and thirty-year-old fliers with hand-drawn maps trying to rally community support for mountain preservation. Looking through the file, it became that much clearer just how many people have dedicated either their free time or professional lives to the Santa Monica Mountains.

Many of these same people were equally generous with their time in helping us put together this book. City of Calabasas planning commissioner and longtime mountain advocate Dave Brown provided invaluable help through interviews and an early look at the manuscript. Jo Kitz at the Mountains Restoration Trust provided a thorough reading and over the years has helped put the uniqueness of the Santa Monicas in context for me. Years ago Suzanne Goode at California State Parks made a passing comment that someone should write a book about the mountains, which helped plant the seed for this project. Her enthusiastic and detailed look at the text was essential.

Park Superintendent Woody Smeck, Deputy Superintendant Lorenza Fong and the staff at Santa Monica Mountains National Recreation Area were instrumental in pulling the book together. Over the years, Jean Bray provided a steady flow of updates and news. Brendan Clarke endured our input as he worked on maps that we hope will help readers better understand the range's geography, while Ray Sauvajot helped with information about mountain wildlife and Mike Malone assisted with movie history. A special thanks should also go to Phil Bedel and Phil Holmes at the recreation area's archive. Their guidance directed us to numerous sources of information and it was always a treat to visit this inner sanctum, never knowing for sure just what surprises awaited.

Thanks also to Rorie Skei at the Santa Monica Mountains Conservancy for her close reading of the text and for the updates on mountain news that she has provided for years. Griffith Park ranger Anne Waisgerber helped with passages on the park while Dr. Michael Zakian of Pepperdine University was generous enough to provide materials related to plein air painting in Malibu. Ken Bernstein at the Office of Historic Resources, Los Angeles Department of City Planning, also graciously looked at sections focused on the mountains' unique architectural history. Dr. Eugene Fritsche, professor emeritus of geology, California State University, Northridge, helped sort out questions about the range's complex geology.

On the visual end, Brian and Michael Shore at Photographics, Inc., Curt Grosjean at The Darkroom, and Van Webster of Webster Communications all contributed greatly to the ultimate quality of the book's images. Thanks also to Susan Petrulas Nissman, senior field deputy to Los Angeles County Supervisor Zev Yaroslavsky, who helped mightily with access to the mountains over the years. Our deepest thanks to Amy Inouye of Future Studio for her sensitive and intelligent design.

Finally, we would like to thank Milt McAuley. His trail guides and wildflower book have long provided numerous ways to discover the mountains for thousands of Southern Californians. He is also the uncle of Angel City Press publishers Paddy Calistro and Scott McAuley. We suspect that the experiences and insights that he has offered Scott and Paddy over the years helped lay the groundwork for their enthusiastic response to Tom's blind pitch for this book. Without their understanding that the time for a Santa Monica Mountains book had truly come, this book may have never happened.

Bibliography

Alleman, Richard. *Hollywood: The Movie Lover's Guide: The Ultimate Insider Tour of Movie L.A.* New York: Broadway Books, 2005.

Apostol, Jane. "Don Mateo Keller: His Vines and His Wines." In *Southern California Quarterly, Summer 2002.* Los Angeles: Historical Society of Southern California.

Bakker, Elna. *An Island Called California: An Ecological Introduction To Its Natural Communities.* Berkeley: University of California Press, 1971.

Banham, Reyner. *Los Angeles: The Architecture of Four Ecologies.* London: Penguin Press, 1971.

Barbour, Michael; Pavlik, Bruce; Drysdale, Frank; and Lindstrom, Susan. *California's Changing Landscapes: Diversity and Conservation of California Vegetation.* Sacramento: California Native Plant Society, 1993.

Bartlett, Dana W. *The Bush Aflame.* Los Angeles: Grafton Publishing Corp, 1923.

Bell, Major Horace. *On the Old West Coast: Being Further Reminiscences of a Ranger.* New York: William Morrow & Co., 1930.

--*Reminiscences of a Ranger or Early Times in Southern California.* Santa Barbara: Wallace Hebberd, 1927.

Brewer, William H. *Up and Down California in 1860-1864: The Journal of William H. Brewer.* Berkeley: University of California Press, 1966.

Bureau of Reclamation, Lower Colorado Region. "Rindge Dam Removal Study: An Effort To Reduce the Decline of the Malibu Creek Steelhead Trout Population in Southern California." Appraisal Report prepared for California Department of Fish and Game, April 1995.

The California Art Academy and Museum in cooperation with The Frederick R. Weisman Museum of Art, Pepperdine University. "On Location in Malibu: Paintings By The California Art Club." Pasadena: California Art Academy and Museum, 1999.

California State Parks. *Will Rogers State Historic Park Historic Landscape Management Plan, Final 3/25/03.*

Capra, Pablo, editor. *Idlers of the Bamboo Grove: Poetry from Lower Topanga Canyon.* Brass Tacks Press, 2002.

Chase, J. Smeaton. *California Coast Trails: A Horseback Adventure from Mexico to Oregon in 1911.* Santa Barbara: The Narrative Press, 2001.

County of Los Angeles Fire Department. *Official Report, Old Topanga Incident,* 1993.

Dailey, Victoria; Shrivers, Natalie; Dawson, Michael; introduction by William Deverell. *L.A.'s Early Moderns: Art/Architecture/Photography.* Los Angeles: Balcony Press, 2003.

Dale, Nancy. *Flowering Plants: The Santa Monica Mountains, Coastal & Chaparral Regions of Southern California.* Santa Barbara: Capra Press, 1986.

Dallman, Peter R. *Plant Life in the World's Mediterranean Climates: California, Chile, South Africa, Australia, and the Mediterranean Basin.* Sacramento: California Native Plant Society and Berkeley: University of California Press, 1998.

Davis, Mike. *Ecology of Fear: Los Angeles and the Imagination of Disaster.* New York: Metropolitan Books, 1998.

Dennett, Preston. *UFOs Over Topanga Canyon.* St. Paul: Llewellyn Publications, 1999.

Dunaway, David King. *Huxley in Hollywood.* New York: Harper & Row Publishers, Inc., 1989.

Dunham, Judith. *Details of Frank Lloyd Wright: The California Work, 1909-1974.* San Francisco: Chronicle Books, 1994.

Eberts, Mike. *Griffith Park: A Centennial History.* Los Angeles: The Historical Society of Southern California, 1996.

Edwards, Ph.D Allan E. *Franklin Canyon: A Microhistory.* Beverly Hills: William O. Douglas Outdoor Classroom, 1994.

Fagan, Brian. *Before California: An Archaeologist Looks at Our Earliest Inhabitants.* Lanham, Maryland: Rowman & Littlefield Publishers, Inc., 2003.

Fine, David. *Imagining Los Angeles: A City in Fiction.* Albuquerque: University of New Mexico Press, 2000.

Flannery, Tim. *The Eternal Frontier: An Ecological History of North America and Its Peoples.* New York: Atlantic Monthly Press, 2001.

Frank Meline Co., Inc. "Bel-Air: The Exclusive Residential Park of the West." Undated promotional brochure.

--"California Riviera." Undated promotional brochure.

Friedrich, Otto. *City of Nets: A Portrait of Hollywood in the 1940s.* New York: Perennial Library, 1987.

Fulton, William. *The Reluctant Metropolis: The Politics of Urban Growth in Los Angeles.* Baltimore: The Johns Hopkins University Press, 2001.

Fultz, Francis M. *The Elfin Forest.* Los Angeles: Times-Mirror Press, 1923.

Gebhard, David. *Schindler.* San Francisco: William Stout Publishers, 1997.

--. *Schindler Architect.* Catalog for An Exhibition of the Architecture of R.M. Schindler, 1967.

Gill, Brendan. *Many Masks: A Life of Frank Lloyd Wright.* New York: G.P. Putnam's Sons, 1987.

Grant, Campbell. *The Rock Paintings of the Chumash.* Berkeley: University of California Press, 1965.

Greene, Linda W. "A Historical Survey of the Santa Monica Mountains of California: Preliminary Historic Resource Study, Santa Monica Mountains National Recreation Area." August, 1980.

Gumprecht, Blake. *The Los Angeles River: Its Life, Death, And Possible Rebirth.* Baltimore: The Johns Hopkins University Press, 2001.

Halsey, Richard W. *Fire, Chaparral, and Survival in Southern California.* San Diego: Sunbelt Publications, 2005.

Hockney, David. *Hockney's Pictures: The Definitive Retrospective.* New York: Bulfinch Press, 2004.

Hollywood Bowl Association, Inc. *Souvenir Program: Grand Dedicatory Benefit Opening of the New Hollywood Bowl.* June 22, 1926.

Hollywoodland Tract Office. *Hollywoodland: Five Minutes From Hollywood's Great White Way* (promotional pamphlet). Los Angeles: Hollywoodland Tract Office, 192?.

Heizer, Robert F. and Elsasser, Albert B. *The Natural World of the California Indians.* Berkeley: University of California Press, 1980.

Heilbut, Anthony. *Exiled in Paradise: German Refugee Artists and Intellectuals in America from the 1930s to the Present.* Berkeley: University of California Press, 1997.

Hise, Greg and Deverell, William. *Eden By Design: The 1930 Olmsted-Bartholomew Plan for the Los Angeles Region.* Berkeley: University of California Press, 2000.

Hoskyns, Barney. *Waiting for the Sun: Strange Days, Weird Scenes, and the Sound of Los Angeles.* New York: St. Martin's Press, 1996.

Huffman, Margaret. *Wild Heart of Los Angeles: The Santa Monica Mountains.* Niwot, Colorado: Roberts Rinehart Publishers, 1998.

Huxley, Aldous. *After Many a Summer Dies the Swan.* New York: Harper, 1939.

Huxley, Laura Archera. *This Timeless Moment: A Personal View of Aldous Huxley.* New York: Farrar, Straus & Giroux, 1968.

Isherwood, Christopher. *Diaries: Volume One: 1939-1960.* New York: Michael di Capua Books, 1996.

--*A Single Man.* New York: Farrar, Straus and Giroux, 1964. New York.

Kaufman, Polly Welts. *National Parks and the Woman's Voice: A History.* Albuquerque: University of New Mexico Press, 1996.

Keeley, Jon. E., Witter, M.S., and Taylor, R.S. *Challenges of Managing Fires Along an Urban-Wildland Interface— Lessons from the Santa Monica Mountains, Los Angeles, California.* Sydney, Australia: Third International Wildland Fire Conference [Proceedings], 2004.

--"Chaparral," chapter in *North American Terrestrial Vegetation,* edited by M.G. Barbour and W.D. Billings. Cambridge: Cambridge University Press, 2000.

King, Chester. *Native American Indian Cultural Sites in the Santa Monica Mountains.* Prepared for the Santa Monica Mountains and Seashore Foundation, February 2000.

Klein, Joe. *Woody Guthrie: A Life.* New York: A.A. Knopf, 1980.

Kroeber, A.L. *Handbook of the Indians of California.* New York: Dover Publications, 1976.

Jones, Jack. Vasquez: *California's Forgotten Bandit.* Carlsbad, California: Akira Press, 1996.

Lamprecht, Barbara. *Richard Neutra 1892-1970: Survival Through Design.* Cologne: Taschen, 2004.

Lillard, Richard G. *Eden in Jeopardy: Man's Prodigal Meddling with His Environment: The Southern California Experience.* New York: Alfred A. Knopf, Inc., 1966.

--. *My Urban Wilderness in the Hollywood Hills.* Washington, D.C.: University Press of America, Inc., 1983.

Los Angeles Fire Department. "The Los Angeles Brush Area Conflagration November 6-7, 1961: Bel-Air-Brentwood and Santa Ynez Fires Worst Fire in the History of Los Angeles." Official Report of the Los Angeles Fire Department Compiled by Capt. Harold W. Greenwood, L.A.F.D.

Louvish, Simon. *Keystone: The Life and Clowns of Mack Sennett.* New York: Faber and Faber, Inc., 2003.

McAuley, Milt. *Wildflowers of the Santa Monica Mountains.* Canoga Park: Canyon Publishing Co., 1985.

McCarthy, John Russell. *These Waiting Hills: The Santa Monicas.* Los Angeles: The Times-Mirror Press, 1925.

McClung, William Alexander. *Landscapes of Desire: Anglo Mythologies of Los Angeles.* Berkeley: University of California Press, 2000.

McCoy, Esther. *Case Study Houses, 1945-1962.* Los Angeles: Hennessey & Ingalls, 1977.

--. *Five California Architects.* New York: Reinhold Publishing Corp., 1960.

McDonough, Jimmy. *Shakey: Neil Young's Biography.* New York: Random House, 2002.

McWilliams, Carey. *Southern California Country: An Island on the Land.* New York: Duell, Sloan & Pearce, 1946.

Miller, T. Christian, "Head for the Hills," article in *The Amicus Journal.* Spring 2000 .

Moure, Nancy Dustin Wall. *California Art: 450 Years of Painting and Other Media.* Los Angeles: Dustin Publications, 1998.

--. *William Wendt, 1865-1946.* Laguna Beach: Laguna Beach Museum of Art, 1977.

Myrick, David F. *The Determined Mrs. Rindge and Her Legendary Railroad.* Ventura: Ventura County Historical Society, 1996.

National Board of Fire Underwriters and The Board of Fire Underwriters of the Pacific. "The Malibu Fires, Los Angeles and Ventura Counties, California: December 26-30, 1956." Undated report.

National Park Service, U.S. Department of the Interior. "Santa Monica Mountains National Recreation Area, California. Final General Management Plan Environmental Impact Statement, Volumes 1 and 2." July 2002.

Northcutt, John Orlando. *The Hollywood Bowl Story.* Hollywood: Hollywood Bowl Association, 1962.

Nunis, Jr., Doyce Blackman. *Andrew Sublette: Rocky Mountain Prince 1813-1853.* Los Angeles: Glen Dawson, 1960.

Ornduff, Robert, Faber Phyllis M. and Keeler-Wolf, Todd. *Introduction To California Plant Life.* Berkeley: University of California Press, 2003.

O'Malley, Penelope Grenoble. *Malibu Diary: Notes from an Urban Refugee.* Reno: University of Nevada Press, 2004.

Ovnick, Merry. *Los Angeles: The End of the Rainbow.* Los Angeles: Balcony Press, 1994.

Palmer-Lacy, Jenifer. *Runyon Canyon Park.* Brochure produced in conjunction with exhibit "Flashback: Fastforward: Past and Future Views of Runyon Canyon," 1993.

Pavlik, Bruce M.; Muick, Pamela C.; Johnson, Sharon G.; and Popper, Marjorie. *Oaks of California*. Los Olivos: Cachuma Press, 1991.

Pitt, Leonard and Pitt, Dale. *Los Angeles A to Z: An Encyclopedia of the City and County*. Berkeley: University of California Press, 1997.

Pyne, Stephen J. *Fire in America: A Cultural History of Wildland and Rural Fire*. Seattle: University of Washington Press, 1997.

Raven, Peter H. *Native Shrubs of Southern California*. Berkeley: University of California Press, 1966.

Raven, Peter H. and Thompson, Henry J. *Flora of the Santa Monica Mountains, California*. Los Angeles: University of California, Los Angeles, 1977.

Rindge, Frederick H. *Happy Days in Southern California*. Cambridge and Los Angeles, 1898.

Rindge, John F. and Rindge, Ronald L. *Andrew W. Sublette Encounters Two Grizzly Bears in Malibu Canyon on December 17, 1853*. Paper submitted as part of application to designate a portion of Malibu Canyon as a California Point of Historical Interest, 1993 and 2001.

Rindge, Ronald L. *Ceramic Art of the Malibu Potteries*. Malibu: Malibu Lagoon Museum, 1988.

-- *The Rediscovery of the Pueblo de las Canoas*. Malibu: Malibu Historical Society and the Malibu Lagoon Museum, 1985.

--. *Letter to U.S. Army Corps of Engineers Re: Public Meeting for the Malibu Creek (Rindge Dam) Ecosystem Restoration Feasibility Study*, May 25, 2002.

Robinson, W.W. and Powell, Lawrence Clark. *The Malibu: Southern California's Famous Rancho, Its Romantic History and Present Charm*. Los Angeles: The Ward Ritchie Press, 1958.

Rogers, Betty. *Will Rogers: His Wife's Story*. Norman: University of Oklahoma Press, 1979.

Rooney, Brian. *Three Magical Miles: An Appreciation of the Past & Present of Malibou Lake & Vicinity*. Agoura, California: Cornell Preservation Organization, 2003.

Roth, Matthew W. "Mulholland Highway and the Engineering Culture of Los Angeles in the 1920s." In *Metropolis in the Making: Los Angeles in the 1920s*. Edited by Tom Sitton and William Deverell. Berkeley: University of California Press: 2001.

Ruthven, Madeleine. *Sondelius Came to the Mountains*. Los Angeles: The Primavera Press, 1934.

Santa Monica Mountains Task Force and Sierra Club. *About the Century Ranch*. Undated pamphlet.

Saunders, Charles Francis. *The Southern Sierras of California*. Boston: Houghton Mifflin Co., 1923.

Schnauber, Cornelius. *Hollywood Haven: Homes and Haunts of the European Emigres and Exiles in Los Angeles*. Riverside: Ariadne Press, 1997.

Schoenherr, Allan A. *A Natural History of California*. Berkeley: University of California Press, 1992.

Secrest, William B. *California Desperadoes: Stories of Early California Outlaws in Their Own Words*. Clovis, California: Word Dancer Press, 2000.

See, Carolyn. *Golden Days*. Berkeley: University of California Press, 1987.

Sennett, Mack. *King of Comedy*. Garden City, New York: Doubleday & Co., Inc., 1954.

Sharp, Robert P. *Coastal Southern California*. Dubuque: Kendall/Hunt Publishing Co., 1978.

Smith, Catherine Parsons. "Founding the Hollywood Bowl." Article in *American Music*, Summer 1993.

Smith, Kathryn. *Frank Lloyd Wright: Hollyhock House and Olive Hill Buildings and Projects for Aline Barnsdall*. New York: Rizzoli, 1992.

Starr, Kevin. *Material Dreams: Southern California Through the 1920s*. New York: Oxford University Press, 1990.

--. *The Dream Endures: California Enters the 1940s*. New York: Oxford University Press, 1997.

Sweeney, Robert L. *Wright in Hollywood: Visions of a New Architecture*. New York: Architectural History Foundation, 1994.

Viertel, Peter. *The Canyon*. New York: Harcourt, Brace and Company, 1940.

Viertel, Salka. *The Kindness of Strangers*. New York: Holt, Rinehart and Winston, 1969.

Walter, Bruno. *Theme and Variations: An Autobiography*. New York: Alfred A. Knopf, 1947.

Weide, David. "The Geography of Fire in the Santa Monica Mountains," Masters thesis, Department of Geography, California State University, Los Angeles, 1968.

West, Nathanael. *The Day of the Locust*. New York: Signet Classic, 1983.

Willard, Daniel E. "The Geologic Story," chapter in *The Pacific Coast Ranges*, Roderick Peattie, editor. New York: The Vanguard Press, 1946.

Williams, Greg. *The Story of Hollywoodland*. Papavasilopoulos Press, 1992.

Wright, Frank Lloyd. *An Autobiography*. New York: Duell, Sloan, and Pearce, 1943.

Yagoda, Ben. *Will Rogers: A Biography*. New York: Alfred A. Knopf, 1993.

York, Louise Armstrong. *The Topanga Story*. Topanga: Topanga Historical Society, 1992.

Young, Betty Lou. *Rustic Canyon and the Story of the Uplifters*. Santa Monica: Casa Vieja Press, 1975.

--. *Santa Monica Canyon: A Walk Through History*. Pacific Palisades: Casa Vieja Press, 1997.

Zakian, Michael. "Historic Landscapes of Malibu," article in *American Art Review*, Volume X, Number 2, March-April 1998.

Index

Front Gallery Photograph Captions

Cover—Marine mists move through coastal canyons and highlight the Santa Monicas' jagged profile in this view looking west toward Boney Ridge.

Page 1—Shaded by coast live oaks, Sulphur Creek flows through Cheeseboro Canyon in the upper watershed of Malibu Creek.

Pages 2-3—A brilliant winter sunset silhouettes Ladyface Mountain in Agoura Hills.

Pages 4-5—The largest of the range's resident birds, the great blue heron is able to take advantage of hunting opportunities in mountain streams.

Page 6—Sycamore roots, acorn and lichen-crusted bark on a streambed; Bottom: Morning mist veils slopes at Paramount Ranch as equestrians head out to explore the longtime film location site.

Page 7—Top: Breaking storm over Simi hills, Bottom right: Valley oak leaves.

Page 8—For all its vistas, much of the Santa Monicas' beauty is found in its details, such as this fungus on a valley oak, that resembles a sea anemone; Acorn woodpecker granary in valley oak.

Page 9—Newly fallen sycamore leaves blanket stream cobbles in Malibu Creek. Fall color displays begin in early November and can run into late December.

Page 10—One of three federally listed endangered species in the Santa Monicas, Bird's Beak grows only at Mugu Lagoon.

Page 11—Flows tumble along massive volcanic boulders covered by years of moss growth at Big Sycamore Creek in Point Mugu State Park.

Pages 12-13—Reddening sycamore leaves stand out against golden grasses as fog lifts from Reagan Meadow, once owned by the late president.

Map Credits

Endpapers: David Rumsey Map Collection, www.davidrumsey.com
Pages 206-207: Brendan Clarke, Denise Kamradt, National Park Service, Santa Monica Mountains National Recreation Area

The Santa Monica Mountains: Range on the Edge
Copyright © 2006 by Matthew Jaffe and Tom Gamache
Photographs © 2006 by Tom Gamache. All rights reserved.

Designed by Amy Inouye, www.futurestudio.com

First edition
10 9 8 7 6 5 4 3 2

ISBN-10 1-883318-51-3 / ISBN-13 978-1-883318-51-2

Library of Congress Cataloging-in-Publication Data

Jaffe, Matthew.
  The Santa Monica Mountains : range on the edge / Matthew Jaffe ; photography by Tom Gamache.
p. cm.
  Includes bibliographical references and index.
  ISBN-13: 978-1-883318-51-2 (hardcover : alk. paper)
  1. Santa Monica Mountains (Calif.)—Description and travel. 2. Santa Monica Mountains (Calif.)—Pictorial works. 3. Los Angeles Region (Calif.)—Description and travel. 4. Los Angeles Region (Calif.)—Pictorial works. I. Gamache, Tom, 1941-. II. Title.

F868.L8J34 2006
917.94'940454--dc22
                                        2006025865

Printed in China

ANGEL CITY PRESS
2118 Wilshire Boulevard #880
Santa Monica, California 90403
310.395.9982
www.angelcitypress.com

MOORPARK

SIMI VALLEY

118

CAMARILLO

101

Calleguas Creek

Simi Hills

Simi Peak

China Flat
2403'

Palo Comado Cyn

Chesebro Cyn

Upper Las Virgenes Preserve (Ahmanson)

Conejo Mtn
1819'

Newbury Park

THOUSAND OAKS

Laskey Mesa

Oak Park

Plain

Calleguas Creek

Rancho Sierra Vista/Satwiwa

Hidden Valley

Lake Sherwood

Westlake

Lake Lindero

AGOURA

WEST LAKE VILLAGE

HILLS

CALABASAS

Big Sycamore Cyn

Boney Mountain State Wilderness Area

Sandstone Peak
3111'

Las Virgenes Res.

Medea Creek

Las Virgenes

La Jolla Valley

Point Mugu State Park

Boney Mtn

Backbone Trail

25

Paramount Ranch

Peter Strauss Ranch

Malibou Lake

Malibu Creek State Park

Gillette Ranch

Cold Creek

Point Mugu Beach

Ray Miller Trailhead

Thornhill Broome Beach

Saddle Rock

Castro Peak
2824'

Tapia Park

Sycamore Canyon Beach

Mulholland Hwy

Leo Carrillo State Park

Trancas Cyn

Zuma Cyn

Kanan Dume Rd

Solstice Cyn

Malibu Cyn Rd

Gorge

Pacific Coast Hwy

County Line Beach

Nicholas Canyon Beach

MALIBU

Pacific Coast Hwy

Dan Blocker Beach

Malibu Surfrider Beach

Malibu Lagoon

Pacific

Ocean

Zuma Beach

Westward Beach

Point Dume